T0355700

"FRIENDS IN PEACE AND WAR"

"FRIENDS IN PEACE AND WAR"

THE RUSSIAN NAVY'S LANDMARK VISIT TO CIVIL WAR SAN FRANCISCO

C. Douglas Kroll

POTOMAC BOOKS, INC.
WASHINGTON, D.C.

Library of Congress Cataloging-in-Publication Data

Kroll, C. Douglas.
  Friends in peace and war : the Russian Navy's landmark visit to Civil War San Francisco / C. Douglas Kroll. — 1st ed.
      p. cm. — (Potomac's military controversies)
  Includes bibliographical references and index.
ISBN-13: 978-1-59797-054-9 (hardcover: alk. paper)
ISBN-10: 1-59797-054-9 (hardcover: alk. paper)
1. United States—Foreign relations—Russia. 2. Russia—Foreign relations—United States. 3. United States—Foreign relations—1861–1865. 4. Russia. Voennyi flot—History—19th century. 5. Warships—Russia—History—19th century. 6. Warships—California—San Francisco—History—19th century. 7. Sailors—Russia—History—19th century. 8. Sailors—California—San Francisco—History—19th century. 9. San Francisco (Calif.)—History, Naval—19th century. 10. San Francisco (Calif.)—Social conditions—19th century. I. Title. II. Series.

  E183.8.R9K76 2007
  973.7′22—dc22

                                                          2006031556

Printed in the United States of America on acid-free paper that meets the American National Standards Institute Z39-48 Standard.

Potomac Books, Inc.
22841 Quicksilver Drive
Dulles, Virginia 20166

First Edition

10 9 8 7 6 5 4 3 2 1

*To Lana, Timothy, and Matthew,
and in memory of Clifford and Martha Kroll*

CONTENTS

ILLUSTRATIONS

PREFACE

For most people, the terms "San Francisco" and "Civil War" have nothing to do with one another. The well-known battles of the Civil War, such as Bull Run, Shiloh, Antietam, Vicksburg, Gettysburg, Chickamauga, and Mobile Bay, all took place east of the Mississippi River. A few might remember that there were some minor battles west of the Mississippi in Missouri and Arkansas, but that is as far west as they think the Civil War extended. San Francisco was separated from the scene of the conflict by hundreds of miles of sparsely settled territory, which included the Great Basin and much desert, and by two great mountain ranges. The city was eleven thousand miles away by sea. San Francisco—and California, although a state since 1850—seemed to be too far from the fighting to be actively involved or play any significant role in the war.

It was late in April 1861 before the news reached San Francisco that Fort Sumter in Charleston, South

Carolina, had been fired on and surrendered on April 14. The fact that it took ten days by a combination of telegraph and Pony Express for word to reach San Francisco says something about how far removed the city was from the action. This did not mean, however, that it would not be involved.

Jefferson Davis and other Southern leaders recognized early the value of gaining the American West for themselves, if for no other reason than securing the western gold and silver regions whose wealth could finance the Confederacy. California's gold would be a particularly valuable prize. Confederates hoped western areas would join them by alliance or by conquest. In July 1861 Confederate troops from Texas crossed over into the New Mexico territory. They advanced to about sixty miles from the Colorado River by the spring of 1862 before being turned back by Union troops sent from Southern California. But although there was not a single Civil War battle, or even a skirmish, in California, San Francisco was an integral part of that war.

From 1861 to 1864, more than $173 million passed through the Golden Gate from the California mines and the Comstock Lode of Nevada. This immense treasure fed the coffers of the Union throughout the war and marked the city and its harbor as a prime target for the Confederacy and its supporters. The treasure was not only badly needed by the Union, it was purposefully kept away from Confederate hands. When the Civil War began, the seven Confederate states had only $27 million in specie. Beyond that lay nothing except the dubious expedients of credit and confidence. Capturing even a single gold steamer leaving San Francisco would have greatly strengthened the Confederacy's credit. San Franciscans knew that their harbor was important because of the gold that passed through it, the U.S. Mint in their city, the nearby Mare Island Naval Shipyard, and Benicia Arsenal.

San Franciscans feared the possible actions of Confederate sympathizers within their midst. An actual plot involving California gold shipments was discovered and thwarted at the last minute with the seizure of the ship *J. M. Chapman* in San Francisco Bay on March 15, 1863. But perhaps San Franciscans' greatest fear was an enemy warship sailing through the Golden Gate and holding the city hostage under its guns. It could be one of the Confederate commerce raiders. It could be a British or French warship, if either country allied itself with the Confederacy and attacked San Francisco.

When the Civil War broke out, the Navy's Pacific Squadron consisted of only six small wooden ships with less than one thousand men manning them. Their job was to cruise the Pacific Ocean protecting U.S. commerce. Although the squadron eventually grew to fifteen ships, its primary task was never to protect San Francisco and its harbor. Fort Point guarded the southern side of the Golden Gate and Fort Alcatraz guarded the harbor. Additionally, an armed government vessel was assigned to the harbor, the small revenue cutter *Shubrick*. Even with these protections in place, San

Franciscans were less than convinced about their city's safety.

As a result, in the fall of 1863, when the Pacific Squadron of Imperial Russia arrived in their harbor, San Franciscans rejoiced. The Russian squadron would remain for almost a year. While these Russian ships had not come primarily to protect the city from possible Confederate attack, they were welcomed with open arms and great relief. This visit would lead to an outpouring of compliments and goodwill from both the Russians and the San Franciscans, which included balls, parades, and dinners. There were historical and practical reasons for these exceptionally friendly relations, and they can only be understood by first knowing about the relationship between these two great nations in the years preceding this important visit.

ACKNOWLEDGMENTS

I incurred many debts to individuals and institutions while writing this book. Among the archivists and librarians who aided my research, I am especially grateful to Mark Porras, Library Specialist/Interlibrary Loan Agent at the College of the Desert Library in Palm Desert, CA; Robert Glass, archivist at the National Archives and Records Administration—Pacific Region in San Bruno, CA; Robert M. Browning Jr. and Scott T. Price, historians at Coast Guard Headquarters in Washington, DC; and Elena Tsvetkovo at the BLITZ office in St. Petersburg, Russia. Staff members at the Bancroft Library of the University of California, Berkley; at the National Maritime Museum's J. Porter Shaw Library, San Francisco; and at the National Archives and Records Administration in Washington, DC, also gave valuable assistance.

Special thanks go to my wife, Lana, for her encouragement and suggestions throughout my research and writing, and to our older son, Timothy, who translated all of the Russian sources for me. His assistance was invaluable.

1

RUSSIAN-AMERICAN RELATIONS AT THE TIME OF THE CIVIL WAR

In the 1860s there were four major military and naval powers in the world: Britain, France, Russia, and the United States. In 1860 Britain was the world's most powerful industrial nation and the British Navy, which had won overwhelming superiority in the Napoleonic Wars, was still without equal in numbers or confidence. None of the powers was more aware of this fact than the United States. The United States had fought two bitter wars against Britain: the War of Independence and the War of 1812. Additionally, the two nations endured many years of tension without war, which frequently concerned border issues in North America. In 1842 they quarreled over the Maine boundary, and in 1846, over the Oregon boundary. A dispute over San Juan Island led to the Pig War of 1859. At the height of that war, 461 Americans with fourteen cannon faced five British warships and 2,140 troops. Before any shots were fired, the nations reached a temporary agreement and maintained token forces on the island until the long-standing dispute was finally resolved in 1872 by the new Kaiser Wilhelm I of Germany.

In 1861, Britain's declaration of "neutrality" at the beginning of the American Civil War was its de facto recognition of the Confederacy as a "belligerent." By doing so Britain refused to recognize the war as an internal conflict and gave the Confederacy the status of a nation for the sole purpose of prosecuting war. However, the Confederacy's search for diplomatic recognition almost lead to another war between Britain and the United States. Two Confederate diplomats slipped out of Charleston in a blockade runner and reached Havana, where they boarded the British mail steamer *Trent* and sailed for Europe. The USS *San Jacinto*, aware of the diplomats' presence in the *Trent*, stopped the vessel on the high seas, took the Confederate diplomats into custody, and delivered them to Boston. The *Trent* was then allowed to proceed to Britain. While Union supporters in the United States rejoiced, the British were outraged. The British government sent the U.S. government an ultimatum demanding an apology and release of the Confederate diplomats. Britain ordered troops to Canada and strengthened its western Atlantic fleet. It also ordered an embargo of all saltpeter shipments to the United States until the crisis was resolved. (Saltpeter was the principal ingredient in gunpowder and was desperately needed by the Union army.) War between the two nations seemed imminent, when President Abraham Lincoln and Secretary of State William H. Seward, who were unwilling to risk war with Britain, released the diplomats with an indirect apology.[1] Still, Britain began the construction and repair of six Confederate commerce-raiding ships—including the *Alabama, Florida,* and *Shenandoah*—in 1862, which further increased bad feelings between the two nations. The United States protested this British action, and after the war it pursued a prolonged battle over damage claims against Britain, known as the *Alabama* claims.

The United States had its share of difficulties with France as well. While France had been a vital ally of the United States during its War of Independence, relations deteriorated shortly afterward. In 1793 the United States quarreled with France about neutrality and then fought a brief, undeclared war in 1798. Tensions arose again over Napoleon's paper blockade of European ports in 1809. In 1831 France agreed to pay the United States indemnities arising out of the illegal captures and detentions of American merchantmen prior to 1800. When France continued to delay payment, President Andrew Jackson threatened war. In 1834 Great Britain intervened and helped settle the dispute, avoiding war. By the time of the Civil War, Americans were complaining about the French occupation of Mexico and that regime's conduct toward the Confederate rebels. Napoleon III had encouraged Maximilian to accept the Mexican throne as emperor, and French troops in Mexico schemed to render military assistance to the Confederacy and reportedly planned to invade Arizona and California.

By contrast, the United States had never had a quarrel or war with Imperial Russia, and, in fact, the relationship was characterized by peace and goodwill. On September 1, 1775, Britain's King George III sent a personal message to Tsarina Catherine the Great to ask for Russian soldiers to help suppress the rebellion of his subjects in North America. King George III hoped to obtain a corps of twenty thousand soldiers, but the tsarina politely but firmly refused his request. After failing to receive Russian support, the British government hired soldiers from sovereign German princes. In addition to refusing to send soldiers to Britain, the Russians also initiated a policy of armed neutrality, to which all European governments adhered, and which helped bring about Britain's isolation.[2] Russia also was one of the first nations to recognize the independence of the United States.

That friendship was evident after the war when the Continental Navy no longer existed, having been disbanded in 1785. In April of 1788, Continental navy officer and hero John Paul Jones traveled to St. Petersburg and accepted an offer to become a rear admiral in the Russian navy, since there was no longer an American navy to serve in. In June 1788, during the Second Russo-Turkish War, he led a Russian squadron that defeated the Turks at the battle of Dneiper Liman in the Black Sea. The tsarina awarded him the Order of St. Anna for his service. Jones departed Russia the following year and died in Paris on July 18, 1792.[3] The U.S. Navy would not be founded until 1798.

During America's involvement in the Tripolitan War against the pirates of the Barbary States of northern Africa (1801–1804), the thirty-six-gun USS *Philadelphia* ran aground in Tripoli harbor and was captured on October 31, 1803. The captain and crew were removed and held as hostages in the city of Tripoli. In 1804 Tsar Alexander I tried to persuade the Turkish government to intercede in hopes of gaining the release of the American prisoners. His efforts were unsuccessful, but following the overthrow of the ruler of Tripoli in 1805, the American prisoners were set free.

In June 1809 the U.S. Senate confirmed President James Madison's appointment of John Quincy Adams as the United States' first minister to St. Petersburg. His wife, Louisa, and their youngest son, Charles Francis Adams, age two, accompanied him. Adams served in that position until 1815 and he became a good friend of Tsar Alexander I. He was in St. Petersburg when Napoleon's *Grande Armée* entered Russia in June 1812. By the middle of September, the *Grande Armée* invaded Moscow, only to find the ancient capital in ruins without shelter for the troops. The winter soon closed in and Napoleon's troops retreated under constant attack by Russian forces. Adams was in St. Petersburg to see Alexander rejoice over the end of the Napoleonic Empire in Europe and to witness the tsar's wartime religious conversion. A short time later, the Russian emperor helped mediate a peace between the United States and Britain to end the War of 1812. Because of Adams' close relationship with the tsar, he was appointed the chief U.S. negotiator at Ghent, where a treaty was signed on Christmas Eve in 1814.

Because of this growing friendly relationship, the United States signed a treaty in 1832 that made Russia the first nation to have "most favored nation" trading status. It would be one of many acts that would strengthen the bond between the two nations.

In the late 1840s an assertive French government claimed rights over sacred institutions in Palestine. These claims raised questions about Russia's protectorate over Christians in the Ottoman Empire, a position that was affirmed in the peace treaty of Kuchuk-Kainardji (1774) but disputed by the Turks. Diplomatic relations between Russia and the Turks continued to worsen in the early 1850s. Tsar Nicolas I decided to intervene in Turkish affairs in hopes of gaining control of the straits between the Black Sea and the Mediterranean. Russia soon occupied the Rumanian-inhabited Turkish principalities of Moldavia (Moldova) and Wallachia. Confident of British and French support, Turkey declared war on Russia on October 4, 1853. In March 1854, after Russia ignored the Turks' demand to evacuate Moldavia and Wallachia, Britain and France also declared war. British and French forces landed in the Crimea in September 1854.

The United States stood alone by Russia in 1854 and 1855 during the ensuing Crimean War. With scarcely a dissenting voice, the American press and public appeared to conclude that the world was picking on its overseas friend, Russia. President Franklin Pierce—the fourteenth president of the United States, who was known primarily for his support of the Kansas–Nebraska Act and the repeal of the Missouri Compromise—all but went to war with Britain and France on Russia's behalf.

U.S. Navy crews rescued the crew of the Russian ship *Diana* in the Far East. The U.S. government furnished Russian forces with arms and sent a whole shipload of gunpowder to the defenders of the Siberian coast. Three hundred Kentucky riflemen offered to go to the Crimea, where volunteer American surgeons were already serving with the Russian forces. Support for Russia ran especially high in California. William H. Gwin won re-election to the U.S. Senate after calling for all-out support for Russia. Beverly C. Sanders, a prominent merchant in San Francisco, offered his services and steamers to Russia. These steamers, if armed, could have swept the Pacific of every French and English cruiser and merchant ship in a very short time.[4]

The Russian Embassy in Washington, DC, was flooded with requests for letters of marque from American citizens who wanted to enter the service of the tsar as privateers against Britain. James Buchanan, later the fifteenth president of the United States and a former ambassador to Russia, served as the U.S. ambassador in London at the time. Buchanan was practically a Russian spy, and he passed on anything he learned to Secretary of State William Marcy, who then relayed it to St. Petersburg through the Russian embassy. The U.S. government allowed Russian-American Company ships built in East Coast shipyards to sail to the Pacific and then run the blockade of Russian America (Alaska) under the U.S. flag.

Frank Golder, no Russophile, would later write of the Crimean War, "By the time it was over the United States was the only nation in the world that was neither ashamed nor afraid to acknowledge boldly her friendship for Russia."[5] The behavior of the United States during this war unquestionably impressed the Russians and strengthened the goodwill between the two nations.

While the Turkish, British, and French residents of San Francisco celebrated the fall of Sebastopol on September 8, 1855, with a parade and rally, far more Americans in San Francisco cheered for the Russians. Later that same day, a large group of San Franciscans held a rally in front of the Montgomery Block, a four-story brick office building on Montgomery and Washington streets, supporting Russia. Following the rally, the crowd marched, accompanied by several bands, to Folsom Street in Russian Hill—a fine residential district of the city supposedly named for the burial place of Russian sea otter and seal hunters on its crest—to serenade the Russian consul and to assure him of their support. The consul was overcome with both joy and gratitude for the American sympathy.[6]

Although the Russian abandonment of Sebastopol in September 1855 to the attacking British-French forces virtually ended the war, the final peace treaty was not signed at Paris until March 1856. Still, the treaty settled none of the issues that brought about the war.

After the war, Tsar Alexander II—who succeeded to the throne in March 1855 when his father, Tsar Nicolas I, died—sent thanks to President Pierce for his kind deeds and encouraging words on behalf of Russia. American naval engineers engaged in raising the Russian vessels that were sunk during the war at various ports of the Black Sea. The Russian forces who were sent to the Crimea were supplied by ox cart because of Russia's late start in railway building, so later, at Tsar Alexander's invitation, American railroad engineers helped the Russians expand their railroad system.

Less than ten years later—during the dark days of the American Civil War—because Russia alone among the three great European powers had given no aid or comfort to the Confederacy, U.S. citizens believed that Russia was the only friend of the Union. Union supporters feared that either Britain or France would enter the war on the side of the Confederacy, and these same Union supporters consoled themselves with the hope that they could count on the aid of the Russians if that happened.

Early in 1861 the French proposed that Russia join them and other nations in intervening in the American Civil War. The Russians declined. Similarly, the

United States declined France's invitation to join the European powers in dictating to Russia about its Polish problem in 1863. The Russians resented Britain and France's threat to intervene on behalf of the tsar's Polish subjects, who were rebelling and demanding independence. Similarly, Americans resented Britain and France's support of the Confederacy. While Britain and France had not officially recognized the Confederacy, by recognizing the South as a belligerent, they permitted it "to solicit loans, contract for arms...send commissioned cruisers to sea, exercise all rights of search and seizure," and send diplomats abroad. Supporters of the Union were angered at Britain's construction and repair of a fleet of commerce raiders for the Confederacy to attack U.S. merchant ships. France had issued its own neutrality proclamation at about the same time as Britain and already occupied the neighboring Republic of Mexico.

Russia, however, displayed a markedly different attitude. In the fall of 1862, the Russian foreign minister, Prince Aleksandr Mikhailovich Gortchakov, assured the U.S. chargé d'affaires, Bayard Taylor, that Russia would not participate in any form of European intervention in the American conflict:

> Russia alone has stood by you from the very
> first, and will continue to stand by you. . . .
> We desire, above all things the maintenance
> of the American Union as an indivisible

nation. . . . Proposals will be made to Russia to join some plan of interference. She will refuse any invitation of the kind. . . . You may rely upon it.[7]

In February 1862, a Confederate diplomat appeared in St. Petersburg. The Russian government not only refused to meet with him, it ordered him to leave. Shortly afterward, a Union emissary, Charles A. De Arnaud, arrived in St. Petersburg. Whereas the Confederate diplomat had been asked to leave, De Arnaud was summoned to the Russian Foreign Office, where Prince Gortchakov inquired if the United States government had sufficient vessels to maintain the efficiency of its naval blockade of the Confederacy. De Arnaud replied that he did not know, and Prince Gortchakov then responded emphatically: "I shall find out whether they have vessels enough to maintain the blockade, and if they haven't we have! The Emperor, my August Master, will not permit any one to interfere with this blockade, even if he has to risk another allied war!"[8] The Russian tsar believed a strong and unified United States, friendly to his nation, would provide an important geopolitical balance to the power of Great Britain.

Of particular interest to those who supported the Union cause was the fact that Tsar Alexander II had issued the Emancipation Manifesto on February 19, 1861, which freed the serfs throughout Russia; President Lincoln issued the Emancipation Proclamation on January 1, 1863, which freed the slaves in Confederate territories that were still in rebellion. Alexander II became known as the "Tsar-Liberator," while Abraham Lincoln was referred to as "The Great Emancipator." The Rev. Starr King, one of San Francisco's leading citizens at the time and a champion of the Union cause, spoke of the tsar as "the Great Imperial Abolitionist of all history." Artemus Ward, in a later lecture, called Alexander "the Starr King of Europe."[9]

Americans were also encouraged by the new reformist tsar's pardon of the Decembrist rebels, who thirty years earlier failed in their coup for reform. Tsar Alexander II instituted trial by jury and a new penal code, relaxed censorship, chartered new industries, and commissioned a railroad to be built to the Black Sea. In addition, he provided for an elaborate scheme of local self-government for the rural districts and large towns of Russia, with elective assemblies possessing a restricted right of taxation. A number of Americans believed that Russia was about to be modeled on the plan of the United States. They saw the Romanovs, especially Alexander II, as the possible reformers of Europe and looked forward to and hoped for constitutional and representational government in Russia.[10]

San Franciscans had even more reason to look favorably on the Russians. In 1861 Russia and the United States agreed to cooperate to establish a telegraph cable connection between St. Petersburg and San Francisco by way of the Bering Sea and Siberia. In his third annual message to Congress, President Lincoln confirmed this program by saying, "Satisfactory arrangements have been made with the Emperor of Russia, which, it is believed, will result in effecting a continuous line of telegraph through the empire to our Pacific Coast." They also hoped that since the Russians had recently taken control of the Amur River and thereby gained a connection between the interior of Siberia and the Pacific— as well as a new port on the Okhotsk Sea—the Amur River would become the St. Lawrence River of the Asian continent and that San Francisco would be the chief port for all trade with what returning whalers had told them was a thriving land of great wealth.

Similar problems and shared potential enemies gave the United States and Russia a common bond, and their history of good relations caused both nations to overlook the differences in language, religion, and political opinions that might have separated them. There were also many similarities between the two nations: Both had risen within the past fifty years to become major world powers. Both covered immense areas of territory. Both were making great economic progress. The two were the largest producers of grain in the world, and America was the chief producer of cotton, while Russia was the chief producer of hemp. Additionally, Russia was third—while the United States was first—among the gold-producing nations.

Now in this critical period of the early 1860s, Russia was fighting against insurrections from its Polish and Caucasian subjects while the United States was fighting a rebellion by eleven of its southern states, which had seceded to form the Confederate States of America. Both nations feared the intervention of Britain or France in what they considered to be internal matters. An editorial in April 1862 in a leading San Francisco newspaper summed it up well: "It must be plain to the most superficial observer, that with the exception of Russia, there is not one nation in all Europe that would not rejoice in the downfall of the American nation. They have all shown themselves in their true colors since the rebellion commenced. It is true that our relations with them, just at this time, are pacific, but no man can tell how long that state of affairs will last."[11]

The Poles had become restless under the political conditions imposed upon them by Tsar Nicolas I, and they expected a change for the better when Alexander II came to the throne. When one year after another passed without any significant improvement, their discontent began to manifest itself in active opposition to the Russian government. This Polish opposition first appeared openly on February 25, 1861, and kept growing during the following two years until finally, in January 1863, the "January Uprising" signaled the open rebellion of the Poles against Russian rule. Owing to the intensive anti-

Russian propaganda carried on by the numerous Polish *émigrés* in various European capitals, the rebellion quickly gained the support of public opinion throughout Europe. Thinking that they could crush the rebellion by seizing the most active leaders of the insurrection, the Russian police arrested these men with the intention of putting them into the Russian army. This act angered Britain and France and made 1863 an exceedingly tense year. For a time, it appeared that a general European war might be a possibility.

Britain, France, Austria, and other powers (with the exception of Prussia) protested to Russia over its treatment of the Poles. On April 17 the representatives of these governments addressed a note of remonstrance to Prince Gortchacov, the Russian minister of foreign affairs. This sharp note demanded the immediate recognition of Poland as an independent nation; however, it did not have the desired effect and was followed by a second in June and a third in August. But the tsar, emulating Lincoln's stand in the American rebellion, declared that the Polish uprising was purely a domestic affair and that foreign intervention was not acceptable. The point of dispute was clear and sharp and could be decided in only one of two ways: either by the Russians or the Poles backing down, or by fighting a war.

Russia expected Britain and France to declare war and thus prepared for its eventuality. Russia had always been a continental power, and the deployment of Russian naval forces had always been constrained by the "tyranny of geography." The majority of Russia's

coastline is in the arctic north; Russia's Atlantic Squadron was in reality its "Baltic Fleet," and its Pacific
Squadron was made remote not only by the distance from
Kronstadt and Vladivostok respectively, but also by the
lack of good supply routes or rapid communication.

By June 1863, war seemed inevitable and while
the Lord High Admiral, Grand Duke Konstantin
Nikolaevich, was at Warsaw, General-Adjutant Nikolai
Karlovich Krabbe, commander of the Imperial Russian
Navy, began to work on a plan. The Russian fleet, recently reorganized, was very weak in comparison with
the fleets of Britain and France. The Russian navy had
been rebuilding since its destruction in the Crimean War,
and it now consisted of the small squadron in the Pacific, the somewhat larger squadron in the Baltic, and a
frigate in the Mediterranean. The ships were all, or
nearly all, made of wood, and although they had steam
engines, their principal means of propulsion was still
the sail (the orders being that steam should be resorted
to only in case of urgent necessity). Krabbe submitted
his recommendations to the emperor on July 5. He noted
that Russia's fleet of small ships could never defend
themselves against the combined naval assault of Britain and France, but on the high seas the situation was
much different. The quickly maneuverable, steam-pro-
pelled Russians ships were more than a match for the
British and French sailing merchant vessels. Krabbe

went on to suggest that as soon as Britain realized what Russia had in mind, it would reconsider intervening in the Polish situation. What Russia feared, however, was that if its fleet remained in home waters, it would probably be blocked in, as it had been during the recent Crimean War. It was therefore necessary for the fleet to be sent to a place more conveniently located for commerce raiding and where it could not be trapped. The ships should leave individually and appear to be destined for the Mediterranean or the Pacific.[12]

Krabbe proposed that two cruiser squadrons of approximately equal strength should be formed and dispatched to Union ports. The Baltic Squadron, based in Kronstadt, near St. Petersburg, should be ordered to New York and the Pacific Squadron, based in Vladivostok, to San Francisco. These two cities were chosen, at least in part, because Gideon Welles, the American secretary of the navy, had offered the facilities of the Brooklyn and Mare Island Navy Yards for the repair and overhaul of the Russian ships. The success of the whole plan depended entirely upon its being carried out quickly and covertly so as not to arouse suspicion. The entire personnel of each squadron were to be selected from unmarried men, because of the length time the squadron would be in the United States.

These arguments appealed to Alexander II and he accepted Krabbe's propositions on July 7. The ships were ordered to prepare themselves for foreign service and to be provided with money enough for two years. The tsar knew that the ships could not remain in Russia and that there was no other place in Europe where they would be received with friendship. If they anchored in the United States, however, they could indeed dash out quickly and in a short time be on the trade routes, acting as privateers, should war break out. Newly promoted Rear Adm. Stepan Lesovskii was given command of the Baltic fleet and ordered to sail his ships to New York. Rear Adm. Andrei Alexandrovich Popov, commander of Russia's Pacific Squadron, had been ordered earlier—in case war broke out between Russia and Britain or France over the Poles—to take his weakest ships to a safe harbor and with those remaining ships to destroy the enemy's commerce.[13] Now, with war imminent, he was ordered to take his squadron to San Francisco as a precautionary measure.

Rear Admiral Popov fully supported taking his ships to San Francisco, which would give independence to his Pacific Squadron and allow it to sail forth to attack British or French ships. Popov wanted to avoid a repetition of the problems of the Crimean War. He firmly believed that one of his ships acting independently could catch or destroy nine merchant ships, seriously damaging Britain's trade. This would offer him the opportunity to take revenge for the British victory at Sebastopol during the recent war. He had visited San Francisco in 1859 and had made many friends; if he brought his squadron there, he was confident of a warm reception.

The port also had the only dry dock for repairing ships on the Pacific Coast—the U.S. Navy's Mare Island Navy Yard. Popov could, of course, take his squadron to one of the Russian stations in the north Pacific, notably those of the Russian-America Company; however, Alaska had neither postal nor telegraphic facilities, nor any means of provisioning and repairing his ships.

Popov left Europe in late January 1862 and arrived in Hong Kong in April. On his way he stopped for port visits in his flagship, the corvette *Bogatyr*, at Melbourne and Sydney, Australia. It was a friendly visit, however a few Australian newspapers expressed alarm over the Russian presence. They suggested that the Russians were investigating coastal fortifications for a possible future invasion of Australia, in case of war with Britain over the Polish Rebellion.[14]

During the trip, Popov sent the ships of his squadron to different places in the Far East, such as China, Japan and the Philippine Islands, to observe the strengths and weaknesses of the European colonies, and also to give his men necessary training in seamanship and long distance cruising. Popov himself sailed from Kamchatka on August 26 to visit Sitka, where he was very critical of the leadership of the Russian-American Company and what he believed was their wasteful spending habits. He then sailed on to Esquimalt, near Victoria, British Columbia, and finally to San Francisco briefly, where he anchored in the last port on September 28, 1862.

On his return voyage to Russia, he stopped at Honolulu, and from there he sailed for Nagasaki, where his squadron was to rendezvous in early November. Upon Popov's arrival in Nagasaki on November 9, he continued preparing his vessels for crisis operations in case of war. During the winter he made other cruises, and with the experience and knowledge Popov acquired, he was in a good position to know how to act when called upon.

He did not have to wait very long. Krabbe wrote to him on April 24 to inform him of the critical situation in Europe and to warn him to be ready at any moment to attack the enemy. Unfortunately, there would not be telegraph or railroad connections between St. Petersburg and Vladivostok for another fifty years. Instead, Krabbe's letter had to be sent by a special courier, who traveled many weeks in order to deliver it. The letter of April 24 finally reached Popov on July 20. On the following day, he replied that he was taking his squadron to San Francisco and ordered a collier to Kodiak Island, Alaska, which he intended to use as one of his bases.[15] Popov ordered the swift clipper *Gaidamak*, which was officially a part of the Baltic fleet, to follow him to San Francisco. Krabbe was indignant over what he considered to be Popov's insubordinate conduct by taking a ship to San Francisco that Krabbe had long ago ordered transferred to the Baltic fleet. The relationship between the two would remain strained throughout Popov's time in San Francisco and would eventually lead to his relief from command while the squadron was still in port there. Russian foreign minister Edouard de Stoeckel officially notified Secretary of the Navy Welles of the Russian fleet's visit in a letter dated September 23, 1863.

❧

The arrival of Russia's Pacific Squadron in San Francisco in the fall of 1863 was welcomed with cheers. One editorial stated: "Cheers for Russia! The shaggy-coated stranger of the northern wilds proved a friend in a region where we scarcely thought of looking for one. May the harmony between the nations be perpetual."[16]

San Franciscans were well aware of the Polish rebellion and read about it regularly in their newspapers. And while they probably realized that the Russian warships did not come primarily to help protect their city, the squadron was welcomed with open arms and great relief. San Franciscans considered the presence of the Russians a confirmation of their friendship and support of the Union cause.

San Franciscans were also probably aware that in June 1861 John Basil Turchin (Ivan Vasilovitch Turchinov), a former colonel in the tsar's army and a graduate of the Imperial Military School in St. Petersburg, and immigrant to the United States in 1856, was serving as a colonel in the Union Army. He would distinguish himself at the Battle of Chickamauga in September 1863 and earn the nickname "The Russian Thunderbolt." Later promoted to the rank of brigadier general, he served until ill health forced him to leave the army in early fall of 1864.

2

SAN FRANCISCO'S FEAR

To better understand how welcome the Russians were in San Francisco, one must first examine in greater detail the feeling of fear that gripped San Francisco's residents at the time.

Although California seemed to be too far from the battlefields of the Civil War to be actively involved, it actually had an anti-slavery record—indeed, slavery had been declared illegal in California in 1829, when it was still a part of Mexico. Still, the state had been a stronghold for pro-Southern Democrats almost continuously since its admission to the Union. Except for a brief Know-Nothing period, Democrats had governed California since its admission in 1850, a fact largely attributable to an active Southern element in the population and particularly to the influence of its aggressive leaders. All of California's representatives in Congress were from the South; in the spring of 1861, when the Civil War began, state and military leaders were all of

Southern origin. The pro-slavery legislature of 1859 had been sympathetic to a proposal for California to secede from the United States and become an independent Pacific Republic. In a letter, Representative John C. Burch went so far as to urge his fellow Californians (in case of emergency) to "raise aloft the flag of the 'bear,' surrounded by the 'hydra'-pointed cactus of the western wilds, and call upon the enlightened nations of the earth to acknowledge our independence, and to protect us, the only 'waif,' from the wreck of our noble Union— the youthful but vigorous Caesarians republic of the Pacific." No less an official than Gov. John B. Weller (1858–1860) had declared that if the nation should divide in a civil war, instead of siding either with North or South, California should establish on the shores of the Pacific "a mighty republic, which may in the end prove the greatest of all."[1]

While the majority of Californians remained loyal to the Union, many deeply sympathized with the South. Almost 40 percent of the state's 380,000 inhabitants were from slave states and only seven out of fifty-three newspapers had supported Lincoln in the 1860 election. The bear flag, as well as palmetto flags honoring South Carolina, flew in a number of California towns. There were those, although a vocal minority, who openly advocated secession for a time. When it became indiscreet, if not actually dangerous, to openly avow sympathy with the Confederacy, expressions of disloyalty to the Union assumed different and subtler forms, which created fear among many of San Francisco's residents.

Two prominent, secret, pro-Confederacy organiza-
tions—the Knights of Columbian Star and the Knights
of the Golden Circle—were believed to number more
than thirty thousand members in 1861. Their organization was complex, with small lodges in various cities
and towns; the initiatory ceremonies and the system of
grips and passwords were elaborate and the oaths were
impressive and binding. By 1864, some claimed the
groups controlled at least fifty thousand members. Both
were well organized throughout the state, but because
they were secret societies, it was difficult to know their
exact strength.

In addition, there was uncertainty regarding the loy-
alty of the commander of federal troops on the West Coast.
The outgoing administration of President James Buchanan
had dismayed pro-Union citizens in November 1860 by
combining the army's Departments of California and Oregon into a single Department of the Pacific, and by giving command of it to Brig. Gen. Albert Sidney Johnston,
a Texan who was suspected of being a Southern sym-
pathizer. Johnston arrived in San Francisco on January
14, 1861, and assumed command of the huge new department the next day.

Despite the Unionists' concerns, Johnston carried
out his duties loyally. Responding to orders from Gen.
Winfield Scott, he brought in troops from some of the
posts in the field to garrison and strengthen San
Francisco's unfinished harbor defenses at Fort Point.
He also transferred ten thousand rifled muskets from
Benicia Arsenal to Alcatraz and ordered the commander

of that island fortress to be on full alert and to defend it "against all efforts to seize it." Nevertheless, shortly after his home state of Texas seceded from the Union, Johnston resigned his commission on April 10, 1861, but he agreed to continue in his post until his successor arrived. When Gen. Edwin V. "Bull Head" Sumner arrived and issued an order definitely assuming command of the Department of the Pacific on April 25, 1861, a great burden of anxiety was lifted from the minds of many loyal citizens.

Early in the war, San Franciscans feared an overland invasion from the south and east. Arizona settlements had little sympathy for the Union, considering it to have abandoned them to the Apaches. On August 1, 1861, the Confederacy annexed what it called "the Arizona Territory, Confederate States of America." In December of that year, Brig. Gen. Henry Hopkins Sibley of Louisiana arrived in the Mesilla Valley of Arizona with artillery and three mounted regiments of Texans. He hoped to tempt the Mexican states of Sonora and Chihuahua to secede from Mexico and join the Confederacy, and his plans also included invading California and raising the Stars and Bars over San Francisco. Toward the end of March 1862, Confederate forces attacked a Union column at Stanwix Station along the Gila River, within eighty miles of California. News of the incident prompted the San Francisco *Evening Bulletin* of April 28, 1862, to say, "The Secesh are bringing the war pretty close." However, after Sibley's defeat at Glorieta Pass, east of Santa Fe, on March 28, 1862, he began a long retreat back to Texas. With his departure, the fear of an overland attack disappeared.

San Franciscans still feared that a fast and determined ship could easily slip through the Golden Gate and seize Mare Island Navy Yard and the Benicia Arsenal. In a letter to the secretary of the navy on April 2, 1863, the commandant of Mare Island Navy Yard advised that the sheriff of Napa County had reported that an organization of Confederate sympathizers was forming in that county, whose purpose was to attack and destroy the shipyard. With the Norfolk Navy Yard, the only large dry dock on the Atlantic Coast, in Confederate hands, there could be little doubt that seizing San Francisco and its nearby Mare Island was at least in the Confederates' plans. The commandant was given authority to erect earthworks for the defense of the navy yard.

Because control of San Francisco Harbor almost ensured control of the Pacific—as well as control of the shipments of California's gold—defending the port city had actually been a concern long before the Civil War. San Francisco was the place of the greatest economic and strategic value on the entire West Coast, and for this reason a large number of the military and naval installations in the West had been concentrated there ever since the United States had taken over the former Mexican region in 1846. Still, San Francisco's residents feared that it could not be successfully defended against an attack in force from the sea.

One of the earliest steps toward defending San Francisco was the rebuilding of Fort Winfield Scott—better known as Fort Point—on the northernmost tip of the San Francisco peninsula, which was also the south side of the Golden Gate. The spot, which had first been fortified by the Spanish in 1775, had been undergoing reconstruction since the mid-1850s. By 1861 the reconstruction was virtually finished. Still, the armament behind its three-foot-thick walls was hopelessly antiquated. When Company I of the Third U.S. Artillery Regiment moved into Fort Point in February of 1861, they became the keepers of a fort without any cannons. It would not receive guns for the casemates or barbettes for nearly three months. Because Confederate sympathizers boasted that they could easily capture the fort, when the first cannons arrived they were placed on the barbette tier facing south, to repel a land attack, rather than north, to fend off an enemy fleet. By the end of 1861, however, additional cannons arrived and were placed in the casements and the barbette facing the channel.

In the fortification strategy commonly known as the Plan of 1850, cannons mounted on the north and south shores of the Golden Gate would use crossfire on enemy ships entering the bay. In addition, the plan called for an ancillary fortification to be established inside the bay on Alcatraz Island.

The strongest of the harbor's fixed defenses was Alcatraz—a 22.5 acre, steep-sided rock island in mid-bay, about 1.5 miles from the city—which had recently been made headquarters of the Department of the Pacific. The first steps toward fortifying the island were taken in 1854, but little progress was made until 1860, when work began to proceed more quickly. On December 30, 1859, Capt. Joseph Stewart, in the command of Company H, Third Artillery, occupied Alcatraz with his troops.

By the time the Civil War started in 1861, Alcatraz had 111 smoothbore cannon, rows of open gun emplacements carved out of the island's slopes, and a fortified gateway—or sally port—that protected the road to the brick citadel that crowned the island's highest point. In addition to its belt of encircling batteries, it had a three-story-high barracks and three bombproof magazines that each held ten thousand pounds of powder. Other buildings included a large furnace for heating cannon balls, and a fifty thousand–gallon cistern for fresh water. In 1863 a writer described Alcatraz as "a prime fortress, garrisoned by 120 soldiers . . . [with] a belt of encircling batteries, a massive brick guardhouse, and a barracks, three stories high, with accommodations for 600."[2] During the war, Alcatraz would also become a military prison, and by the end of the war more than four hundred soldiers would be stationed on the island, with cannon batteries guarding nearly every side. The latest weapons-—including the smoothbore, twenty-five-ton Rodman cannon that shot fifteen-inch, 440-pound cannonballs as far as three miles—were installed in 1864.

Both Fort Point and Alcatraz artillery were to be ready for instant action. If any vessels were spotted flying the Confederate flag, they were to be immediately stopped or "fired into and sunk." Still, San Francisco's military commanders were not very confident. In September 1862 Capt. William A. Winder complained that Alcatraz's storehouses were not sufficient enough in number, his prisoners were too numerous, and his water supply was too insecure in the event of any enemy attack.[3]

Additionally, the fortification of the north shore of the Golden Gate at Lime Point was never completed. Work would not begin until 1868 and was suspended soon after the initial excavation began. The landowner of Lime Point and the government could never agree on a price, and the fort was never built. The Plan of 1850 also called for the construction of an inner-line of batteries located inside the Golden Gate, including defenses on Angel Island and at Point San Jose; however, cannons were not mounted at either site until 1864.

In 1861 a U.S. Army inspection of the harbor's defenses was so dismaying that it was not made public. It revealed that the harbor was short at least two hundred guns and the appropriate ammunition, that it needed at least 1,550 artillerymen to man its defenses, and that most of the defenses had yet to be built.

❦

When the Civil War began, the U.S. Navy's Pacific Squadron, under the command of Flag Officer John B. Montgomery, consisted of the screw-sloops *Lancaster*, *Narragansett*, and *Wyoming*; the side-wheel

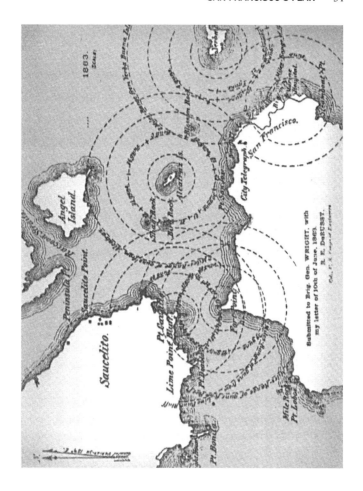

**1863 U.S. Army map of San Francisco Bay
showing gun ranges**

sloop *Saranac*; and the sailing sloops *St. Mary's* and *Cyane*. None of these six vessels, however, were in San Francisco, but rather they were scattered all over the Pacific Ocean to protect merchant shipping. Traveling at the rate of nine to thirteen knots, they cruised along the coast from San Francisco to Panama, sailing as far north as Alaska and as far south as Chile. They visited Hawaii to guard the U.S. whaling fleet, and along the coast of China and Japan they protected U.S. commerce from piratical Chinese junks. Even Australia and the South Seas were included in their itineraries, but homeland defense was not one of their missions.

Acting Rear Adm. Charles H. Bell—who took command of the U.S. Navy's Pacific Squadron from Montgomery on January 2, 1862—described San Francisco's defenses in a letter he addressed to Secretary of the Navy Welles on April 4, 1862. He noted that there was only one fort on the southern side of the harbor entrance (Fort Point) and none on the northern side, but that Alcatraz Island was fortified. Bell who was familiar with San Francisco from his previous service with the Pacific Squadron aboard the *Vincennes* and the *Dolphin* in the 1830s, argued that in the event of war with a maritime power, a few large steamers could easily pass the forts. "[T]he City of San Francisco is Key to the whole of California and this place, once in the possession of a formidable power, the State might be lost to the Union."[4] Admiral Bell recommended assigning a single steam-ram to the harbor, with a few heavy guns mounted on it.

Rear Adm. Charles Bell, Commander of U.S. Navy's Pacific Squadron

About twenty-five miles northeast of San Francisco on an arm of San Pablo Bay was Mare Island Navy Yard, which was founded by Adm. David Farragut in 1854. Nearby was the Benicia Arsenal, which also dated from the 1850s, and which when the war began housed large stores of arms, ammunition, clothing, food, and military supplies. The presence of these installations in themselves would have made San Francisco and its environs a tempting prize to an enemy power—particularly the Confederacy—but within the city itself were other treasures: the U.S. Mint, the customhouse, and the post office were all likely to contain gold and silver that the Confederacy desperately needed.

In an attempt to provide more protection to the city, in October 1863 the secretary of war ordered Gen. George Wright, commander of the Army in the Pacific, to take military possession of Point San Jose "and erect the battery for its defense." Point San Jose was located on the north shore of San Francisco, near Alcatraz Island, and a company of the Ninth Infantry was sent to occupy it. Eventually, a twelve-gun battery was placed on the western side of the point, in position to intersect the shots fired from Alcatraz. The company of infantrymen was finally replaced late in 1864, when a battery of the Third Artillery was transferred from Alcatraz.

Angel Island, the largest island in San Francisco Bay at more than 640 acres, would also be fortified. Camp Reynolds—named in honor of Maj. Gen. John Reynolds, who had been killed in action in the Battle of Gettysburg—was constructed late in 1863, and three artillery batteries were completed by late July 1864 at Points Stewart, Knox, and Blunt. In February 1863 Commodore Thomas Selfridge, commandant of Mare Island Navy Yard, suggested placing a battery of guns at Rincon Point on Yerba Buena Island. This would allow crossfire on any vessel that might get past Alcatraz on the city side.[5]

In his report to Gov. Leland Stanford of December 3, 1863, California's adjutant general, William C. Kibbe, advanced a novel plan for the protection of San Francisco harbor. He proposed that revolving towers be constructed on each side of the Golden Gate. He specified that these towers be one hundred feet in diameter and pierced for two tiers of guns, allowing ample space for thirty guns in each tier. Casemated guns were planned for the foundations of the towers. After completion of the towers, massive chains were to be laid across the Golden Gate. These chains, when raised by windlasses operated by steam engines, would check the speed of any enemy vessel and bring it under the fire of the guns in the towers. Adjutant General Kibbe argued that if the proposed plan were followed, any navy in the world would be prevented from entering San Francisco harbor.[6]

San Franciscans wanted a major warship to defend their harbor and city, and this desire was recognized on February 3, 1863, when Commodore Selfridge acknowledged a telegram from the secretary of the navy that authorized the use of the *Independence*, then at Mare Island, "or any other measures necessary for the protection of the City of San Francisco from attack."[7] The 190-foot *Independence* was the first ship-of-the-line commissioned in the U.S. Navy. Launched on June 22, 1814, in the Boston Navy Yard, the *Independence* had served in the War of 1812, a war with the Barbary pirates, and the blockade of the Mexican coast during Mexican War. She had briefly served as flagship of the Pacific Squadron from 1855 until 1857, when she entered Mare Island Navy Yard to serve as a receiving ship. She remained there until she was decommissioned in November of 1912. The old *Independence* was obviously not suited to guard San Francisco harbor, so Commandant Thomas Selfridge wrote to Secretary of the Navy Gideon Welles on behalf the city's citizens, stating that because "apprehensions exist in regard to the passage of a rebel steamer by the forts in San Francisco Harbor in a fog, or in a dark night, I deem it important that a man of war be anchored in those waters to cooperate with the forts against attack, and to afford protection to that part of the city lying beyond the range of the fort's guns."[8]

Several months later, Selfridge sent another request to the secretary of the navy: "The mercantile community of San Francisco has expressed much anxiety in regard to the disturbance of commerce on this coast by rebel steamers, and in consequence of this expression I was induced to say in my telegram that more steamers were required to check privateering. If there could be a larger naval force of steamers in these waters it is very probable that it would deter, at least, the equipment of privateers."[9]

Acting Rear Adm. Charles H. Bell reinforced Commandant Selfridge's concerns. In reporting his intended departure from Callao, Peru, for San Francisco to Secretary Welles, he wrote, "I am anxious to get there (San Francisco), as soon as other duties permit, to hasten the repairs of the *Saranac* and *Cyane*, and to afford protection to the city and its vicinity until other means are provided."[10]

Still, Secretary Welles stubbornly opposed withdrawing vessels from the blockading squadrons to guard any city against what he considered largely imaginary perils; he diverted only a few ships from blockading southern ports to scour the seas in search of Confederate raiders. San Franciscans believed throughout the war that ships of the U.S. Pacific Squadron were more frequently seen at Panama or Valparaiso than at San Francisco, because at the beginning of the war Welles had ordered the commander of the Pacific Squadron to concentrate his force on the route of the mail steamers from San Francisco to Panama, and not on protecting San Francisco Harbor.[11]

The only armed government vessel available to protect San Francisco was the revenue cutter *William L. Marcy*, under the command of Capt. William Cooke Pease. A ninety-four-foot topsail schooner, the *Marcy* had arrived in San Francisco in 1854. In April 1861, following the firing on Fort Sumter, Secretary of the Treasury Salmon P. Chase ordered that the *Marcy* be fit for sea "for the purpose of overhauling vessels supposed to be contraband of war, or owned by members of the Confederate states." That same month the *Marcy* sailed up the Bay of Martinez to Mare Island for extensive repairs and new armament. It soon became apparent that the cost of repairs would exceed what it had cost to build the vessel. In August 1861 the lighthouse tender *Shubrick*, a side-wheeler, was transferred from the Lighthouse Service to the Revenue Marine Service. The *Shubrick* was built in 1857 in the Philadelphia Navy Yard as the first steam tender for the Lighthouse Board and was assigned to the Pacific Coast. The side-wheel steamer was named for the president of the Lighthouse

Service, Capt. William B. Shubrick, who had distinguished himself at several battles in the War of 1812. Although the *Shubrick* was transferred to the Revenue Cutter Service in August 1861 as a wartime measure, she would be returned to the Lighthouse Board in 1867.

The *Shubrick* was made of live and white oak with copper and iron fastenings. At 140 feet and eight inches long, twenty-four feet wide, eight feet deep, and weighing 339 tons, the *Shubrick* carried a crew of thirty-five. Although she was rigged as a brigantine, with her forward mast fully rigged and her mizzen gaffed, the *Shubrick* carried a 284-horsepower "harp and steeple," single-expansion steam engine, which turned the side paddlewheels and could push her up to ten knots in speed. The *Shubrick* had a wooden hull made of Florida live oak and white oak and was painted black with a white boot top stripe, just below the gunwales. The paddle wheels, more than nineteen feet in diameter, were painted red; the paddle boxes were painted white; and the bowsprit, mastheads, yards, and gaffs were black. She had two masts and could carry a jib, a square sail, a fore spencer, a topsail, a mainsail, and a storm trysail. The *Shubrick* originally carried guns to protect it and light stations from Native Americans. Her armament included two twelve-pound guns, two twelve-pound brass Dahlgren guns, one twenty-four-pound brass Dahlgren gun, one thirty-pound Rifled Parrott gun, thirty rifles, fifty-one Colt Navy pistols and holsters, forty-five new cutlasses, thirty old cutlasses, and twenty-four boarding pikes.

In November 1861, Captain Pease assumed command of the *Shubrick*, taking with him the crew of the *Marcy*. The *Shubrick* towed the *Marcy* and anchored it off of the Jackson Street Wharf, where Pease transferred two brass guns and equipment from the *Marcy* to his new ship. In March 1862 the *Marcy* was transferred to the Coast Survey.

For most of the remainder of the Civil War the *Shubrick* would act as the guard ship for San Francisco harbor; however, in addition to this duty, the *Shubrick* also carried out its normal peacetime duties of assisting vessels in distress, putting down mutinies, and enforcing the revenue laws.

The small *Shubrick* seemed inadequate to defend San Francisco from an enemy warship that might pass through the Golden Gate. Not only did San Franciscans fear enemy warships but also privateers fitted out in French-occupied Mexico or British Columbia. British and U.S. troops occupied San Juan Island jointly because the northern boundary was still in dispute, and the British reinforcement of Vancouver Island, which included fourteen warships in the Pacific in 1862, had ignited fears that the British forces might attempt to seize California while the United States was preoccupied with the Civil War in the east.

U.S. Revenue Cutter *Shubrick*

San Francisco's worries were substantiated in February 1863 when the *Victoria Chronicle* printed the story of a group of Rebels who had plotted to seize the *Shubrick*, then in Puget Sound. Their aim was to use the ship to intercept the mail and treasure steamers off the California coast. The *Shubrick's* captain became aware of the plot, ferreted out his own crewmembers who were in on the plan, and tossed them in the jail in Port Angeles, Washington.[12] *Shubrick* spent part of her time in the Puget Sound area during the war and was transferred to the Navy Department in February 1865 for ninety days of special service in the Bering Strait, to support survey operations conducted by Col. Charles S. Buckley, the agent of the Russian Telegraph Company. The Revenue Cutter Service would not return the *Shubrick* to the Lighthouse Board until December of 1866.

From time to time during the war, in the midst of this fear, U.S. Navy warships visited San Francisco harbor, although usually to stop at Mare Island Navy Yard for repairs. One of the first of these ships was the USS *Lancaster*, which arrived on March 7, 1862, for overhaul. The *Lancaster*, a relatively new first-class screw-sloop, was flagship of the U.S. Pacific Squadron. Launched by the Philadelphia Navy Yard in December 1857 and commissioned on May 12, 1859, the *Lancaster* was a 235-foot screw-sloop-of-war. The *Lancaster* was a *Hartford*-class steam sloop, with significantly greater dimensions and displacement than the rest of the ships in that class. She mounted twenty-four broadside nine-inch guns, plus two pivots, and was the only vessel to have a complete spar deck throughout her career. After sailing around Cape Horn, the *Lancaster* reached Panama Bay in December 1859 and became the flagship of the Pacific Squadron until 1866, cruising along the coast of South and Central America, Mexico, and California to protect American commerce and the Pacific mail steamers.

While the *Lancaster* was still in the shipyard at Mare Island, the smaller second-class steam sloop *Wyoming* arrived. Shortly afterward, a telegram arrived from the Navy Department—over the newly completed transcontinental telegraph line—advising that a Confederate raider had appeared in the China Sea, and ordering the *Wyoming* to hunt it down if possible. The *Wyoming's* overhaul was cut short, repairs were rushed to completion, and she sailed for Manila a month later. Much to the chagrin of San Francisco's residents, the *Lancaster* sailed out of the Golden Gate on June 28.

The 155-foot side-wheel steamer *Saginaw* also arrived while the *Lancaster* was at Mare Island. Launched in 1859 as the first vessel of the "long line of ships" built by Mare Island Navy Yard, the *Saginaw* had initially served in the East India Squadron. She returned to Mare Island in July 1862 for repairs, and was recommissioned on March 23, 1863, and attached to the Pacific Squadron. The small, side-wheeled *Saginaw*—the first steamship in the Pacific Squadron—visited Puget Sound that spring to investigate reports that Southern privateers were being outfitted in British Columbia, but she returned after learning that the scheme had no chance of success.

San Franciscans breathed a little easier on February 16, 1863, when the 132-foot sloop, the USS *Cyane*, arrived at San Francisco under the command of Lt. Commander Paul Shirley. The *Cyane* was the oldest vessel in the Pacific Squadron—launched in 1837—and she possessed the most illustrious and colorful record. She had been present when Commodore Thomas Catesby Jones prematurely raised the U.S. flag for Monterey in 1842, and again four years later when formal possession of California was taken during the War with Mexico. From 1850 to 1858, she served in the Atlantic. The *Cyane* rejoined the Pacific Squadron in 1859 and would remain there until decommissioned at Mare Island Navy Yard on September 20, 1871.

The *Cyane's* orders were to anchor in a location that would enable it to defend a portion of the city that could not be covered by the guns of Fort Alcatraz, and to remain there until relieved by the *Saginaw*. At last, it seemed, a navy warship would be defending the city and its harbor, and the *Cyane* would be present to help foil a plot by Confederate sympathizers in the area.

The 2,200-ton USS *Saranac*, built in 1848, arrived in San Francisco on June 8, 1863, and as with most navy ships, she proceeded to Mare Island for ammunition loading. The *Saranac* would remain at Mare Island until March 19, 1864, and thus would be of little help in defending the harbor.

About a year earlier, around the middle of 1862, a group of Confederate supporters in San Francisco decided on a daring plan that would help the Confederate cause. Their plan was to buy a fast-sailing vessel, man her with a crew of adventurous young Southerners, and after secretly arming her, slip out of harbor before federal authorities discovered what was going on. Once on the high seas, they planned to intercept and capture one of the Pacific Mail Steamship Company vessels, which carried California's gold to the East Coast. They would transfer their armament to the captured ship and continue on their way, acting as a Confederate privateer and attacking every Union merchant vessel they encountered.

The plan would not be attempted until after February 17, 1863, when the privately owned schooner *J. M. Chapman* arrived in the city from New York (in the record-breaking time of only 130 days). A former Kentuckian named Asbury Harpending—who only a few months earlier had traveled overland to Richmond, Virginia, via Mexico, to meet with Jefferson Davis—was very interested in this fast schooner. Harpending had shared with Davis his grand plans for raising a rabble army in the gold fields and capturing the Sacramento River steamers; Benicia Arsenal; the Mare Island Navy Yard and the ships there; then San Francisco's forts, and eventually all of California. According to Harpending, Jefferson Davis was impressed enough to give him blank letters of marque and a commission as captain in the Confederate Navy. Harpending avoided the long, slow overland trip on his return and boarded a blockade runner, which took him to the Isthmus of Panama, where he crossed over and returned to San Francisco on a northbound mail steamer. After his return to San Francisco, Harpending and his fellow conspirators began looking for a suitable ship with which to carry out their plan. When the small but fast *Chapman* arrived, they decided to purchase it.

Harpending purchased the schooner, hired a crew, and hauled supplies aboard. Inside boxes labeled and destined for a mining company in Mexico were enough arms and ammunition to fight a small revolution—or possibly to take San Francisco. To avoid suspicion, Harpending had a Mexican friend purchase the arms and ammunition. Unfortunately for him, the skipper he hired for the *Chapman* talked, and his words soon reached interested ears. Lt. Commander Paul Shirley, commanding officer of the USS *Cyane*, and his Marine officer, Lt. Charles H. Daniels, prepared and armed two boatloads of Marines. Other persons kept a close watch on the *Chapman* from the steamer *Brother Jonathan*, which was moored nearby. The California Steam Navigation Company's tug *Anashe* worked up a full head of steam, ready to chase the *Chapman* if the vessel made a run for it.

On Friday night, March 15, 1863, Harpending and his crew moved aboard the *Chapman*. The talkative skipper, William C. Law, was still ashore, drunk. When the planned midnight departure time arrived and Law was still not aboard, Harpending finally concluded that he had turned against the cause, and Harpending prepared to make a run for it. But no sooner had the schooner left the pier than he discovered two boats full of Marines in hot pursuit. The *Cyane's* guns aimed at the *Chapman* and the little *Anashe* came steaming out, full of local police and government officials, including Ira P. Rankin, the customs collector. In a few moments, so many people were on the *Chapman* that there was hardly room for them all.

A search of the *Chapman* revealed not only arms and ammunition, but also incriminating documents. Harpending and his two chief conspirators were arrested; shortly afterward, the tardy Law arrived, paddling out from the beach in a drunken haze. He was just in time to join the rest of *Chapman's* crew on their ride to the military prison on Alcatraz, where they were held incommunicado. They were later transferred to the Broadway jail in San Francisco, where the twenty crewmembers were locked up briefly and then released. Preliminary questioning of Harpending and his crew led authorities to believe that other Confederate privateers might be on the prowl in the Pacific, which caused a stir in San Francisco.

***

The capture of the *Chapman* and the uncovering of the plot to convert her into a privateer to raid Union commerce in the Pacific created excitement and fear among San Francisco's residents. It also strengthened their belief in the need for a U.S. Navy man-of-war to protect the city. The commandant of Mare Island Navy Yard sent an official letter to the secretary of the navy arguing that the capture of *Chapman* was "conclusive evidence of the importance of having a vessel of war, at all times, lying off the city of S.F."[13] The seizure of the *Chapman* got attention not only in San Francisco, but also up and down the Pacific Coast. A newspaper in Olympia, Washington stated:

> The recent seizure of a vessel designed as a rebel privateer [the *J. M. Chapman*] . . . leaves no reasonable doubt of the existence of a secret organization on this coast which

has for its object the aid of the Southern cause
. . . A number of letters were found in the
vessel . . . The following letter throws some
light on the Victoria [*Shubrick*] scheme . . .
'There is no vessel up here that would answer your purpose, unless you could get the
U.S. Revenue Cutter *Shubrick*, which would
be somewhat of a difficult operation, as Uncle
Sam keeps a sharp lookout on things up
here.'[14]

The *Chapman* incident caused San Franciscans
to think again of the exposed state of their harbor. Rumors spread that other privateering vessels were being
fitted out to prey upon California commerce or attack
the city. Articles about the harbor's lack of defenses
and the danger from within and without appeared in
city newspapers on almost a daily basis for several
months, all the time heightening the anxiety of city residents. The *Alta California* expressed the opinion of
many San Franciscans when it printed an editorial entitled "Our Danger," which stated in part:

some pirate, fitted up like the *Chapman*, gets
out of the harbor, captures one of our steamers, transfers her armament to her and pro-
ceeds to prey upon our commerce; or it may
be a rebel privateer envelopes herself in
smoke and during the prevalence of fog en-
ters the Golden Gate and makes her way

around the harbor to Goat Island; or, it may be, moves on with the tide of a star-light night, hugs the shore closely opposite Fort Point, and gains the inside of the harbor unnoticed. What would then be the result? A demand for five millions [*sic*] of dollars could not well be resisted. A bombardment of an hour would set the town, as it is for the most part built of wood, on fire in fifty places. If a high wind—not at all improbable in summer—should be added, there is no power that we possess that would be sufficient to save San Francisco from destruction a third time.[15]

A few days later, the *Alta California* stated in another editorial titled "Our Defences": "We are separated a long way from succor in case of need. We must depend on ourselves in great measure, exposed to pirates, from within and without, and traitors all around us."[16]

On July 1, 1863, in response to recent events, the secretary of the treasury issued an order that no vessel—other than a steamer or packet known to be engaged in regular lines, or in the employ of the army or navy—would be allowed to leave a U.S. port, including San Francisco, between the hours of sunset and sunrise. Additionally, all vessels would have to report to the revenue cutter or guard ship before proceeding to anchorage. The responsibility for enforcing this new regulation fell to the *Shubrick*,[17] and the officers of the

Shubrick were to see that these port regulations were "strictly observed."[18]

From that time on, with the exception of occasional absences of a few days on business connected with the Customs House, the little steamer *Shubrick* would be anchored at her post, midway between Meiggs' Wharf (between Mason and Powell streets) and Fort Point, patiently waiting—"Micawber like"—for something to turn up. A system of signals was arranged between the commanding officer of the *Shubrick* and the officers at Fort Point and Alcatraz, by which the approach of a hostile vessel or fleet could be quickly communicated.[19] Sometimes mistakes were made in the different interpretation of these signals by the officers of the forts and those on the *Shubrick*. On one occasion, by the misreading of a signal from Alcatraz Island, the *Shubrick* went on a cruise of some forty-eight hours in search of a suspicious vessel that no one had ever seen.[20] San Franciscans' fear was so great that on more than one occasion false alarms were given of the approach of an enemy that was to annihilate the vessels in the harbor and the city entirely.

On August 18, 1863, an unidentified vessel was sighted outside the Golden Gate. She was said to be cruising back and forth, as though laying in wait for an incoming or outgoing vessel. The rumor spread through San Francisco that a Confederate commerce raider had taken up position outside the harbor. Inside the harbor, off Black Point, the *Shubrick* cleared her deck for action. Guns were loaded and seamen stood their stations, and the little cutter sailed out through the Golden Gate to investigate the report; she came steaming back. A disgusted Capt. Charles M. Scammon reported that the vessel was a whaler engaged in the legitimate pursuit of its business.[21] At another time, heavy black smoke was seen in the neighborhood of the Farallones Islands, and the vigilant officers of the *Shubrick* put to sea to find—after a sixty-mile cruise—that another innocent whaler was "trying out" prior to landing his cargo at San Francisco's wharfs.[22]

The *Shubrick's* former revenue tasks remained, and in many respects they took on increased importance. Since 1860, tariffs had gone up consistently until, by 1864, they had risen about 47 percent. The North's war effort depended on the collection of custom duties from foreign trade,[23] and collecting them was as important to the *Shubrick* as was her guard-ship duties. And guard-ship duty was not without its risks. On the night of April 20, 1864, the *Shubrick* collided with the barque *W. H. Gawley* from Puget Sound. The *Shubrick* had her starboard anchor broken and a portion of her prow stove in.[24]

The summer of 1863 was a dismal time for Union supporters. Gen. Joseph Hooker had launched an offensive against the army of northern Virginia in early May, only to have it result in the Confederate victory at Chancellorsville (Virginia) at the cost of 17,278 killed, wounded, and missing Union soldiers. By June, Gen.

Robert E. Lee was driving his army northward into Pennsylvania and Confederate commerce raiders, lead by the *Alabama*, *Shenandoah*, and *Florida*, were destroying a large number of Northern merchant ships. A crew detached from the *Florida* that summer raided coastal shipping from Cape Hatteras in North Carolina to Portland, Maine.

During the summer and fall of 1863, the activities of these Confederate raiding cruisers reached their zenith, and numerous Union ships were destroyed in the Atlantic. In August of that summer the Confederate raider *Alabama* reached the South African coast and entered Cape Town. The following month, she sailed into the Indian Ocean, capturing Union ships. The *Alabama* then moved to the Far East to strike at Union traffic in the China Seas, arriving at Singapore on December 21, 1863. The success of these Confederate cruisers not only damaged the Northern maritime trade, it also spread panic to coastal cities like San Francisco.

This was especially true after San Franciscans learned of the daring Confederate raid into Portland harbor in Maine. On July 27 Lt. Charles W. Read, a 23-year-old Confederate navy officer, and his crew quietly sailed into the harbor disguised as fisherman in the captured fishing schooner *Archer*. His plans were to seize one of the two large steamers—*Forest City* or *Chesapeake*—that sailed between Portland and New York, or, failing that, to seize the revenue cutter *Caleb Cushing*. His goals also included attacking Portland and planting the Confederate flag on Maine territory. Because the one engineer in Read's crew told him it would be impossible for him to handle as large a steamer as the *Chesapeake*, Read decided to seize the *Cushing*, a schooner armed with twelve- and thirty-two-pound guns and with only about a third of her crew aboard. At 1:30 a.m. Read and his men rowed across the harbor with muffled oars and swarmed over the *Cushing*, placing the acting commanding officer, Lt. David Davenport, and his men in irons, and then set sail. Due to the light wind, Read put two boats over the side and began to tow the *Cushing* out of the harbor. The *Archer* followed. Once out of the harbor and past Fort Preble, the Confederates hoisted sail while the *Archer* limped behind.

The following morning produced very light winds, and Read discovered to his dismay that he was being pursued by two auxiliary warships and three tugs loaded with soldiers from Fort Preble and a number of armed citizen volunteers. Protected from the *Cushing's* guns by fifty bales of cotton, the *Chesapeake* closed with the stolen cutter. The *Cushing* soon ran out of ammunition and could no longer defend herself. Lieutenant Read put Lieutenant Davenport and his crew of twenty into one of her boats, while his own crew left in the vessel's remaining boats. Read then torched the *Cushing*, which blew up and sank early that afternoon,[25] and he and his men were quickly captured.

The raid on Portland made front-page news across the nation. When the news reached San Francisco, the fear increased that something similar might happen there. A Confederate raider, or Confederates disguised as merchant sailors, might enter San Francisco harbor and carry out a similar raid.

Aware of this possibility the *Alta California* would say in its August 1 edition:

> The port of San Francisco, although so far removed hitherto from the seat of war, is at this moment liable to attack from one or more of the piratical craft of the rebels, which have inflicted such an incalculable amount of damage on the high seas and in the harbors of the ocean. Our comparatively defenseless condition has been for a long time known to the Government at Washington, and through the earnest and indefatigable exertions of our Congressional delegation, together with the hearty cooperation of influential Californians, we are at last in a far way of getting this great harbor on the Pacific coast, securely protected. In yesterday's issue, we noticed the fact of the immediate construction of earthworks in the inner bay. So far, so good; but for the large expanse of water lying between the "bar" and the city, additional protection is needed beyond the fortifications at Fort Point and Alcatraz.[26]

The article went on to discuss the government contract for the *Camanche* and to describe the monitor. The two hundred–foot, eight hundred–ton iron vessel was to be built on the East Coast, then disassembled and shipped to San Francisco for reassembly. San Franciscans desperately wanted an ironclad monitor to protect their harbor, as U.S. Navy vessels were only occasionally in port. This meant that at times the *Shubrick* was the only armed government vessel in the harbor. San Franciscans breathed a collective sigh of relief on Tuesday, September 16, when the USS *Lancaster* arrived back in port.[27] The U.S. Navy's Pacific Squadron had sailed from San Francisco on July 26, 1862, and had been gone for nearly fourteen months visiting the coast of Mexico and South America. Commanding the *Lancaster* was Commodore Joseph Lanman, who had previously commanded the steamsloop *Saranac* in the Pacific Squadron. The *Lancaster*, a 3,250-ton vessel with a complement of three hundred men, could defend the city from any attack. Unfortunately, like most the of the navy's warships, the *Lancaster* had not returned to guard the harbor, but rather for repairs at the Mare Island Navy Yard.

With the *Lancaster* now in port, the *Shubrick* could steam to Mare Island on October 16 in order to receive another cannon, a thirty-pound rifled Parrott pivot gun. This easy-to-operate and durable gun was placed on the forecastle, the rails having been cut down and ports made so that it could be worked abaft the beam and nearly in a straight line. This gun could, in case of emergency, prove to be a very effective "peacemaker." The *Shubrick* returned on October 26 to her old anchorage off Black Point.

San Franciscans were especially frightened during the winter of 1863, when it was reported that the Confederate cruisers *Sumter* and *Alabama* were planning to attack the city. But by that time their fears were somewhat lessened by their knowledge that Russia's Pacific Squadron was now in their harbor and that the Russians appeared to be willing to help fight Confederate forces should they attack the city. Admiral Popov, as commander of the Russian squadron, was aware of the reports about the *Sumter* and *Alabama*, and took measures to prevent the attack. He issued orders to the officers of his squadron that should such a Confederate raider enter the port, the ranking officer of the squadron should at once give the signal "to put on steam and clear for action." At the same time, an officer should be dispatched to the Confederate cruiser to hand its commanding officer the following note:

> According to the instructions received from His Excellency Rear-Admiral Popov, commander in chief of His Imperial Majesty's Pacific Squadron, the undersigned is directed to inform all whom it may concern, that the ships of the above mentioned squadron are bound to assist the authorities of every place where friendship is offered them, in all measures which may be deemed necessary by the local authorities, to repel any attempt against the security of the place.

If no attention was paid to this warning and the Confederate vessel should open fire, it should be ordered to leave the harbor, and in case of refusal it should be attacked.[28]

Copies of these orders were sent to General-Adjutant Krabbe in St. Petersburg and to the Russian ambassador, Eduard Stoeckel, in Washington. Ambassador Stoeckel responded in his letter of March 13 to Popov, explaining that as far as Russia was concerned, there was neither North nor South but one United States, and therefore Russia had no right to interfere in the internal affairs of another nation—Popov should keep out of the conflict. Stoeckel went on to say that it seemed the Confederate cruisers aimed to operate only in the open sea and it was not expected that cities would be attacked. What the Confederate corsairs did in the open sea did not concern Russia; even if they fired on the city's forts it was Popov's duty to be strictly neutral. But in case a Confederate raider passed the forts and threatened the city, Popov would then have the right—in the name of humanity, and not for political reasons—to prevent this misfortune. Stoeckel hoped that the naval strength of the squadron would bring about the desired result and that Popov would not be obliged to use force and involve the Russian government in a situation that it was trying to avoid.[29]

While most San Franciscans probably hoped that the Russian ships would protect them from attack, they welcomed the Russians on a national level for a much different reason. They realized that Russia did not

require the assistance of the United States in its conflict with the Poles any more than the United States
needed Russia's help to crush the rebellion of the Confederacy. However, both nations wanted Britain and
France not to intervene in these conflicts; the friendship, or even an alliance, between the United States and
Russia was for the primary purpose of preventing the
intervention of Britain and France.

3

THE RUSSIANS ARRIVE

Having rendezvoused in Nagasaki, the ships of Russia's Pacific Squadron were sent individually with secret orders to sail for San Francisco, but the first vessel to arrive suffered misfortune. The Russian steam-propeller corvette *Novick*, under Captain-Lieutenant Konstantin Grigorovich Skryplev, departed China on September 1, 1863, and after a twenty-six day voyage across the northern Pacific Ocean, she arrived off the coast of California. Cloudy weather had prevented celestial observations for a number of days, and from dead-reckoning calculations, the *Novick's* officers believed her to be twenty-five miles from the shore. At about five o'clock on the morning of September 26, in a very dense fog, the *Novick* struck a sand bar near Point Reyes. Captain Skryplev immediately ordered the engines reversed in an attempt to back the vessel off the sand bar, but a very heavy sea running toward the shore made his efforts futile. It soon pushed the *Novick* broadside on the beach, in from five to ten feet of water. Skryplev ordered all hands to abandon ship and to head for the nearby beach in the ship's small boats.

The *Novick* wasn't the first shipwreck off Point Reyes, nor would it be the last. On November 4, 1595, Sebastián Rodríguez Cermeño's ship, the *San Agustín* out of Cavite in the Philippines, was driven ashore by a squall and wrecked at approximately the same place on the California coast. On October 27, 1841, the Mexican ship *Ayacucho* ran aground on a sandbar near Point Reyes. In 1852 the *Oxford*, an English merchantman, ran aground near what was to be known as Keys Creek. In 1861 the *Sea Nymph*, a clipper ship believing she was heading for the Golden Gate, and with all sails set in a thick fog, also ran to her doom on Point Reyes Beach. The *Novick* was the fifth ship to end its career off Point Reyes, and at least five other vessels would later run aground and be lost at this treacherous point off the northern California coast.

Captain Skryplev quickly dispatched one of his officers to notify the Russian consul in San Francisco. The lieutenant immediately headed for San Quentin, a distance of about thirty miles. Once there, he found a boatman named Charles Driscoll, who offered to row him to the city. Upon arriving the Russian lieutenant contacted the Russian vice consul, who notified W. B. Farwell, the customs collector for San Francisco, of the disaster. Farwell quickly gave orders for the *Shubrick* to proceed to the scene of the shipwreck and render assistance.[1]

The Revenue Cutter Service (alternately known as the Revenue Marine) had been in existence since 1790 as a part of the Treasury Department, and it was established initially to prevent smuggling, thereby preserving the custom duties that were badly needed for the operation of the new nation. Revenue cutters were also to aid any ship in distress, and the *Shubrick* was the logical choice for this mission. Well-equipped to rescue a grounded vessel, she carried a twenty-eight-foot-long gig on deck—modeled after a whale boat—with two masts, two lug sails, and oars. She also carried two small, twenty-seven-foot-long cutters and a seventeen-foot-long dinghy, each with single masts and sails. The *Shubrick* could also carry two thousand barrels of provisions, twelve hundred gallons of water, seventy-five tons of coal, and four cords of wood.[2] Her first mission as a revenue cutter in San Francisco was to seek two vessels in distress, said to have gone aground off San Francisco in Half Moon Bay in January 1862. She found only one of them—the Dutch schooner *Alpha*—wrecked on the shore near Spanish Town. The *Shubrick* rescued the crew and one lady passenger.[3] The following month, the *Shubrick* came to the assistance of the *Flying Dragon*, which ran aground on Island Rock near Little Angel. Later that same month, the *Shubrick* assisted the steamer *Nevada*, her bow high and dry on the beach near Rio Vista,[4] and in April 1862 the *Shubrick* towed the clipper ship *Sierra Nevada* off Fort Point.

At the time of the *Novick's* disaster, the *Shubrick* was under the command of Lt. Charles M. Scammon. Scammon had taken command in the spring of 1863 while the *Shubrick* was still at Port Townsend. An experienced seaman, he had been a highly successful whaling officer before becoming an officer in the Revenue Cutter Service. At about six o'clock in the evening, as soon as the Russian lieutenant from the *Novick* and the Russian vice consul and agent of the Russian-American Company in San Francisco, Martin Fedorovich Klinkovstrem, were onboard, the *Shubrick* got up steam and proceeded to Point Reyes. The *Shubrick* arrived on the scene at eleven o'clock that night and found the *Novick* a total wreck. She then fired a gun and bore up for Drake's Bay, where the officers on the beach made a signal that they were all ashore except for one man, who was drowned when a lifeboat capsized. The *Shubrick* anchored at Drake's Bay at one o'clock in the morning. Captain Scammon, with the Russian vice consul and the lieutenant from the *Novick*, departed the *Shubrick* immediately, proceeded across land, and arrived at the wreck at three o'clock to find that a small piece of the stern was all that remained of the Russian vessel. Everything that was movable was saved. From four o'clock in the morning to one o'clock in the afternoon, the crew of the *Shubrick* took on board items belonging to the *Novick*. At eight o'clock in the morning, the crew procured some teams to transport the officers' baggage, but they did not have teams enough and the men were compelled to carry their hammocks.

The *Shubrick* returned to San Francisco, anchoring at Meiggs' Wharf at 10:20 p.m., with 160 officers and men from the wrecked *Novick*. A few minutes later, the Russian vice consul, the commanding officer of the *Novick*, and Captain Scammon all went ashore. At eleven o'clock a schooner came alongside the *Shubrick* and took on board all the officers and crewmembers of the *Novick*. By two o'clock the next afternoon, the *Shubrick* had returned to her guard station off Black Point.

The following evening, *Shubrick* returned to Point Reyes to take on board the balance of the crew—eight men and one officer—who had been left as a guard for the wreck until the vessel could be legally disposed of by the vice consul at San Francisco. On the evening of October 1, the *Shubrick* returned to San Francisco with the remaining men and the effects saved from the wreck. These included two loads of sails, in addition to the bedding and baggage.[5] Commenting on the arrival of the Russians, the *Daily Alta California* stated: "We learn that the *Novick* is the van vessel of the Russian fleet under the Russian Admiral Popoff [*sic*], who is shortly expected here with the remainder of his vessels. In times like the present, this hegira, as it were, of the [Tsar's] vessels to this port from Japan, attests their friendly feelings for the great Republic of the western world."[6]

The arrival of the Russian squadron was good news in an otherwise discouraging time. San Franciscans following the war back east had learned of one sickening military disaster after another—Fredericksburg, Chancellorsville, and Chickamauga. The disheartening news of the bloody rout at Chickamauga (September 19–20, 1863), with sixteen thousand casualties killed,

wounded, and captured, had hardly reached San Francisco before the Russians began to arrive. Many undoubtedly thought that just as the French had come in
1778 to help the struggling colonies win their independence from Britain, so now the Russians were making
common cause against Britain and France. Apparently,
the Russians were also welcomed for social reasons.
Under the caption "Warships Coming," the *Daily Alta
California* related, "Fashionable ladies are much elated
at the prospect of a large collection of warships, with a
host of officers in this harbor."[7]

In addition, San Franciscans hoped to have a telegraph to St. Petersburg through Russian America
(Alaska) and Siberia. They rejoiced at every indication
of friendship between the two nations. Shortly after the
arrival of Admiral Popov's squadron, the *Alta California* published an article entitled "Russian Civilities."
In the article, Captain Redfield of the brig *Susan
Abigail*, which had recently arrived in San Francisco,
reported that his vessel had been severely damaged in a
storm and needed repairs. As a result, he put into a
Russian port on the northwest coast. Before he could
secure the necessary workmen, or even make his wants
known, the generous Russian citizens sent aboard a car-
penter and a blacksmith, who went to work with a will
and quickly finished their work. He went on to state
that the Russian workers refused to receive any com-
pensation for their labor. The local townspeople sent
aboard fresh milk and provisions, including a bullock,
and they, too, refused any offer of payment.[8]

On October 1 Captain Skryplev and the officers of the ill-fated *Novick*, together with the Russian vice consul, united in a public expression of thanks to W. B. Farwell and the officers of the *Shubrick* for their efforts and attentions in the relief of their wrecked vessel. A few days later on October 6, the *Novick's* officers held a dinner at the Stevenson House at 1214 Clay Street in honor of Captain Scammon and his officers, Farwell, and other officials, in recognition and appreciation of the many favors that had been extended to them after the disaster at Point Reyes. The wreck of the *Novick* continued to stay in the news throughout the fall. In late October a San Francisco paper reported:

> From parties lately from the wreck of the Russian war steamer *Novick*, at Point Reyes, we learn that the hull of the vessel has broken up. The stern portion has drifted along the beach for nearly a mile, while the bow part has entirely gone to pieces. The wreckers have got some very heavy chains attached to the middle part, which contains the boilers and engine. By using purchases, aided by the occasional high surf, they have drawn it up on the beach about 100 yards nearer high-water mark, which renders it nearly certain that they will save the boilers and engine. They have already got from the wreck all the rigging, sails and spars; also a large brass gun, with carriage complete, and three rifled iron

guns [forty-eight pounders] with sufficient carriages to mount the same. At a lost estimate, it is supposed that the value of the property already saved will exceed $15,000.[9]

In late November the brig *Timanbra* arrived from Drake's Bay, bringing a considerable number of items saved from the wreck of the *Novick*. Among the remains was a rifled brass twenty-four-pound gun and complete carriage, with a quantity of shells and balls. Four iron, forty-eight-pound long-range guns, together with their ammunition, were also recovered. Additionally, there were numerous pieces of machinery, copper sheathing, bolts, and other salvageable material. All of these articles, except for the portions of the steam engines, were to be sold at auction.[10] Early in December a number of the cannons were purchased, but at extremely low prices by private parties on speculation.[11]

Shortly after the arrival and wreck of the *Novick*, San Franciscans bid goodbye to the old sloop *Cyane* as she sailed on a cruise to Mexico and Central America on her way to Panama. The *Cyane* was to replace the *St. Mary* as the guard ship for the Panama Railroad. The day after the *Cyane* sailed, the USS *Lancaster* arrived in the bay, and on September 29 she proceeded to the Mare Island Navy Yard.

Rumors that Confederate warships were operating off the coast were common and did little to soothe

the already tense nerves of the San Franciscans. While the *Shubrick* was out of the harbor rescuing the *Novick*, an incident took place that convinced many of the city's residents that the war had come to their very doorsteps. On the morning of October 1, an hour or two before dawn, residents were awakened by the sound of gunfire, which seemed to come from inside the Golden Gate. Listening to the cannonfire, which continued for some time, they concluded the Confederate cruiser *Alabama* had forced her way into the harbor and was bombarding either Alcatraz Island, or the city, or both.

Daylight revealed the real cause of the commotion. An unidentified warship had sailed through the Golden Gate and entered the harbor, and because there was no wind, the sails and flag hung limp and men and rowboats had to tow the ship. Unlike most merchant vessels, this one did not head toward the city docks. Instead, it was traveling toward Angel Island in the direction of Mare Island and the army arsenal at Benicia. With the guard ship *Shubrick* gone, the commanding officer at Alcatraz assumed guard duty to make sure that no hostile foreign warships entered the bay. Capt. William Winder, the commanding officer, ordered his men to fire a blank artillery charge as the signal for the unidentified ship to stop. The rowboats, however, continued pulling the ship toward the North Bay. Winder then ordered his men to fire an empty shell toward the bow of the ship, a universal challenge to submit to local authority. The shot skipped over the water, passing within three hundred yards of the unidentified ship and dashing water spray on her. The ship halted and responded with gunfire of her own, which Captain Winder confirmed was a twenty-one-gun salute. Through the smoke, the troops on Alcatraz could finally see the British flag waving on the HMS *Sutlej*, the flagship of Adm. John Kingcome, commander of Her Majesty's Naval Forces in the Pacific. Winder ordered his men to return the salute, and it was more than likely this exchange of gun salutes that awakened the city.

Soon messages were exchanged for gunfire. The British admiral was not pleased with his reception in San Francisco. Captain Winder explained his actions by saying, "The ship's direction was so unusual I deemed it my duty to bring her to and ascertain her character." Admiral Kingcome did not accept the explanation as satisfactory, but before General Wright could answer his complaint, the *Sutlej* sailed from San Francisco. The U.S. Army's commanding general of the Department of the Pacific offered the disgruntled British admiral an apology through the British consul, but advised him that he had ignored the established procedures for entering a foreign port during war. The commanding general supported Captain Winder, but later gave him a gentle reminder to act cautiously. Captain Scammon of the *Shubrick* also notified the commanding officer of the *Sutlej*, through the British consul, that to prevent a possible future accident, he should pass between Alcatraz and the cutter in the night. Captain Scammon gave the same advice to the Spanish war steamer *Resolucion*, which was then in port. The *Sutlej* departed San Francisco on October 12.

Meanwhile, the citizens of San Francisco must have been proud of the readiness and alertness of the troops on Alcatraz. Some probably thought that Captain Winder had saved the day, considering that Britain favored the Confederacy. The incident also reinforced the importance of the revenue cutter *Shubrick*'s station near the Golden Gate, in order to assist Fort Point and Fort Alcatraz in guarding the harbor entrance and identifying entering ships.

On October 11, the trial of the *Chapman* conspirators began, which was reported in detail in the local papers and read with interest by the public. The trial reminded them of the possible threats to their safety and the safety of San Francisco. Some pro-Union elements in the city had wanted the conspirators tried for piracy, which was a capital crime. Instead they were indicted for high treason, which also could result in the death penalty, although the usual sentence was long-term imprisonment in addition to a heavy fine. The trial made national news, and the *New York Times,* in writing of the conspirators, said that the trial "showed conclusively that they were provided letters of marque signed by Jefferson Davis."[12]

In the midst of all this, the first Russian warship arrived in the bay. On Monday, October 12, the flagship *Bogatyr* arrived from Olga Bay and anchored in San

Francisco's harbor. She flew the distinct Russian naval ensign, a white rectangle with a light blue saltire. This Andreevsky (St. Andrew) naval flag was familiar to most San Franciscans, as both the *Bogatyr* and the *Abrek* had visited the port in the fall of 1862. The Russian naval flag was designed by Peter the Great and featured the blue cross of St. Andrew, the patron saint of Russia, on a white background. A similar blue and white pennant flew from the main truck, which also included the blue St. Andrew's cross.

The *Bogatyr* had departed Olga Bay thirty-three days earlier. Aboard the 2,200-ton propeller corvette was Rear Admiral Andrei Alexandrovich Popov, commander of Russia's Pacific Squadron. The *Bogatyr*, launched in 1860, carried forty-eight guns and 312 men.

Russian Steam Corvette *Bogatyr*, flagship of the Russian Squadron

Andrei Alexandrovich Popov, born in 1821, entered the Russian navy in 1837. He served at Sebastopol (1854–1855) and was promoted to rear admiral in 1860 while serving in the Baltic. His personal flag—similar to the Russian naval ensign, but with a red stripe at its bottom—also flew from the *Bogatyr*. One historian of the Russian navy describes this commander of the Pacific Squadron: "the 'terrible Admiral Popov,' a fine technician and drillmaster, long-term commander of the Pacific Fleet, a man whose unreasonable demands were legendary. His ships were taut rather than happy, but by demanding the impossible he actually obtained a high measure of smartness and efficiency."[13]

The *Shubrick*, being the only official vessel in port, represented the United States in an exchange of salutes with the *Bogatyr*, and Captain Scammon fired

**Rear Admiral Andrei A. Popov, Commander of
the Russian Squadron**

his cannon fifteen times.[14] Upon arrival Admiral Popov immediately contacted the Russian embassy in Washington, DC, so that it could notify the U.S. government of his fleet's presence in an American port.[15] Admiral Popov was no stranger to San Franciscans. He had visited the city in 1859 and again in 1862, and he had made many friends who welcomed him back. One of Admiral Popov's first responsibilities was to investigate the grounding and loss of the *Novick* under the command of Captain Skryplev. Popov knew Skryplev well, having previously sailed with him aboard the *Bogatyr*, and he knew him to be a cautious sailor. Popov's official report blamed the grounding and wreck on faulty maps that Captain Skryplev had been given. He also noted that the northern California coast was often treacherous and not always clear due to frequent fog. Captain Skryplev's map indicated that there was a lighthouse on Point Reyes, when in fact none existed there. The U.S. Lighthouse Board had attempted to erect a lighthouse at Point Reyes as early as 1855, but owing to a dispute over land ownership it had given up its efforts. Stubborn landowners demanded $25,000 of the federal government for the lighthouse site, a price that was considered highly excessive at the time. An agreement was finally signed in 1869 when 120 acres were obtained for $6,000; a lighthouse was built there and lit for the first time on December 1, 1870. The only lighthouses near San Francisco Bay at the point of the *Novick*'s wreck were Southwest Farallon Light, thirty miles off the Golden Gate; Fort Point and Bonita Lights on each side of the Golden Gate; and Alcatraz Island Light within the bay itself. Captain Skryplev had no reason to suspect the shallowness of the water at the time of the grounding, because the faulty maps aboard the *Novick* did not indicate this. Admiral Popov even blamed himself for not ensuring that the vessel had accurate maps before getting underway. Popov concluded that Captain Skryplev was not responsible for the loss of the *Novick*, but instead that he merited commendation. He also noted that not one sailor was lost, or one trunk, or one sailor's hammock.[16]

Russian officers and sailors soon became a common sight in the city. Their uniforms stood out and, like the Germans, Russian officers and men were always in uniform from morning until night, wherever they went. The Russian officers' uniforms were blue in winter and white in summer and they consisted of a frock coat, the ordinary "reefer" jacket (a close fitting, double-breasted coat of heavy cloth that ended just below the waist) worn buttoned, and the "monkey jacket" (a shorter, waist-length jacket tapering to a point in the back, much like a modern navy mess jacket). The cap was peculiar, rather high and full with a red band. For full parade dress and other formal occasions, all officers wore cocked hats. Under their coats, officers wore a high-buttoned white waistcoat together with a black necktie.

Another difference of the Russian officers' uniforms was the distinguishing marks for ranks. Rather than wearing stripes on their sleeves, officers' ranks were differentiated by shoulder straps or full dress epaulettes. Lieutenants had no fringe on their dress epaulettes, a captain had a plain epaulette with fringe, and Rear Admiral Popov would have worn a shoulder stray with a single eagle or a dress epaulette with a single eagle to indicate his rank.

The Russian sailors' uniforms were not unlike that of other nations. They wore caps similar to those worn by the British and American sailors, a flat hat, with very long ribbon tails. Under the ordinary sea-service jumper or jacket they wore blue-and-white-striped jerseys. The collars of their jumpers or jackets had blue and white stripes, and in the case of white summer clothing, there were also blue stripes on the cuffs. Corporals in the Russian navy wore the sailors' uniforms, but with peaked caps rather than the ordinary sailors' caps. During the winter, officers and men both might wear over their shoulders and down their backs a wool cape with long ends over the chest.

For their part, these Russian sailors found San Francisco to be a city of contradictions and inconsistencies. Facing the plank-paved streets and boardwalks of the business district were three-, four-, and five-story buildings built of brick and stone—their facades decorated with elaborate cast-iron ornaments—right next door to dilapidated shacks. They found beautiful churches not far from saloons and taverns. Thanks to the gold that continued to come from the 1859 Comstock Lode mining, San Francisco was thriving economically. It was also growing rapidly. By the time the Russians arrived, the city's population had reached approximately 120,000, more than doubling since the beginning of the war. Even before the war, it had become the largest American city west of the Mississippi River. New buildings were going up at the rate of two thousand every year, and among them were hotels, theaters, and business blocks. The city had more than one hundred schools, a dozen daily newspapers, forty-one churches, twenty-six theaters—and more than two hundred saloons. Three city railroads ran to Center Street and another railroad was under construction to Lone Mountain Cemetery.

On October 12 the trial of the *Chapman* conspirators came to an end. The jury took just four minutes to find all three men guilty of high treason. A few days later, they were brought into court and sentenced to ten years' imprisonment and fined $10,000. The report of the verdict and sentencing brought an end to this high profile incident and served as another reminder of the danger from Confederate sympathizers within San Francisco.

The day after the trial ended, Admiral Popov paid an official call on Captain Scammon and the *Shubrick*. The admiral was rowed in a gig from his anchored flagship and was received by Captain Scammon with all the honors due a high-ranking naval officer of tsarist Russia. Once on board, the admiral expressed his pleasure at being in San Francisco and at the kindly feelings toward his native land from the Americans. He departed about an hour later and returned to his flagship.

The following morning, the *Shubrick* sailed to Mare Island Navy Yard for the installation of a thirty-pound Parrot rifled gun. The *Shubrick* also transported several officers of Admiral Popov's staff to Mare Island, where they would make arrangements for repairs to the Russian vessels in port. After rounding Mare Island and coming into view of the shipyard, the *Shubrick* hoisted a Russian flag from its foremast and anchored off the yard. Captain Scammon went with the Russian officers to call on Commodore Thomas Selfridge, the commanding officer of the navy yard. The Russian officers also called on Rear Adm. Charles H. Bell, commander of the U.S. Navy's Pacific Squadron, onboard the USS *Lancaster*.

Meanwhile, many of the Russian sailors were enjoying their time in San Francisco—especially in its saloons. Four of these sailors were arrested on October 15 for "intoxication" and placed in jail. The following day they appeared in a courtroom and were released into the custody of a Russian naval officer. The magistrate was undoubtedly pleased to release the sailors, lest he disturb the friendly relations that existed between their nation and the United States. In reporting the incident a local paper commented, "The proprietor of one of our large drinking saloons informs us that the favorite beverage of the 'tars' of the [Tsar] is an admixture of ale and gin! No wonder our Russian visitors find themselves in the Calaboose, after imbibing such a villainous concoction of fluid."[17]

❧

On October 16, the Russian steam corvette *Gaidamak* arrived in San Francisco harbor after a voyage of thirty-four days from Nicolaevski on the Amur River. The 1,050-ton vessel, with a 250-horsepower steam engine and 166 officers and crew, was under the command of Captain Aleksei Alekseevich Peshchurov. The *Gaidamak*, launched in 1849, carried seven guns for armament. Two days later, the Russian steam warship *Kalevala* arrived, eighteen days after leaving Honolulu. The *Kalevala*, launched in 1857 and under the command of Captain-Lieutenant Fedor Nikolaevich Zheltukhin, carried fifteen guns, 196 men, and displaced 1,800 tons. Upon entering the harbor, she saluted Fort Alcatraz and the other Russian vessels in the harbor.

Less than a week later, on October 21, the USS *Lancaster* returned from Mare Island and anchored in San Francisco harbor. The flagship of the U.S. Pacific Squadron was saluted with thirteen guns by the three Russian warships already anchored there, and she returned the salute. The *Lancaster* was then able to provide protection to the city. The following day, Admiral Popov paid a call on the *Lancaster*. Also, as proof of their sympathy with the Union cause, the Russian officers in the harbor handed over $155 in gold to the Russian vice consul for him to forward to the widows and orphans of Union soldiers. On October 23 Admiral Bell and Commodore Joseph Lanman, commanding officer of the *Lancaster*, visited the *Bogatyr*.[18]

The Russians' response to a disastrous fire in San Francisco's financial district the next day would further endear them to the city's residents. At about 1:30 on the morning of October 23, a fire began in the rag store belonging to a Mr. Charley Orley. Before it was extinguished, almost an entire block of wood buildings fronting Davis Street and adjacent to the waterfront was destroyed. The value of the buildings and their contents amounted to more than $100,000. Upon seeing the fire, Captain Petr Afanasievich Chebyshev of the *Boygatyr* sent nearly two hundred men to assist. Each of the men came ashore with a bucket, and the Russian officers offered their services to the chief engineer of the city's fire department. The chief engineer asked the sailors to put down their buckets and go to work manning the pumps on the fire engines, and they responded with enthusiasm and continued until they were almost exhausted. They took a few minutes for rest and resumed their positions on the engines. One article written in November 1863, by Albert P. Wheelan, noted:

> The [city] firemen say they were losing the battle, and that unless they conquered the fire the city would be doomed. The firemen began

to succumb through the hard work they were forced to do with the hand engines and the great heat. They dropped from their places one by one and several engines went out of commission.

Suddenly the spectators began to cheer, and to cheer again and again. A thousand throats took up the cheering. The firemen were electrified when they observed boatload after boatload of Russian sailors and their officers landing with buckets and other fire fighting instruments. . . . They took the places of the tired and exhausted firemen and worked hard and long at the pumps and finally conquered the fire.[19]

Many of the Russian sailors were burned or maimed fighting the fire. One had an arm dislocated, and another's hand was badly crushed. After the fire was extinguished, the sailors accepted the hospitalities of Broderick Engine Company No. 1 at the firehouse. The following day, David Scannell, chief engineer of the city and county of San Francisco, sent the following letter of thanks to Admiral Popov and his men, which was also published in local papers:

To His Excellence Admiral A.A. Popoff, [*sic*] Commanding H.I.M. fleet in the Pacific and China Waters:

Dear Sir: On behalf of myself and the Fire Department of the city of San Francisco, I tender to you our sincere thanks for the generous and efficient service rendered by yourself, officers and men, in assisting us during the disastrous fire on the morning of the 23rd instant. The Department which I have the honor to command, will, in common with the citizens generally, ever retain in grateful remembrance, the noble and heroic conduct of Admiral Popoff [*sic*] and the officers and men under his command.

Very truly, yours, etc.

David Scannell,
Chief Engineer, S.F.F.D.

At about the same time, local citizens were learning of the Russian sailors who were injured fighting the fire, and they started gathering contributions and suggested that gold medals bearing suitable inscriptions be prepared and presented to the injured sailors. Barry and Patten's Saloon at the southeast corner of Montgomery and Sacramento became the collection center for the funds. On the evening of October 26, the San Francisco County Board of Supervisors adopted a resolution which presented the thanks of the city and county to Admiral Popov; Captain Chebyshev; and to the officers and men under their command, for the timely and efficient services so nobly rendered by them in the recent disastrous fire. The clerk of the board of supervisors, James W. Bingham, later presented a handsomely engrossed copy of the resolution to Admiral Popov, who forwarded it to St. Petersburg with a covering letter. A copy of the resolution, signed by the president and clerk of the board and authenticated by the official seal of the city, was also transmitted to each of the officers named in the resolution.

While no documentary evidence has yet been located to establish it as fact, it has long been believed that six Russian sailors who were buried at Mare Island in 1863 were sailors who died as a result of injuries sustained while fighting the October 23 fire. Beside three graves each marked as an unknown "Russian Sailor" are the graves of Russian sailors Artemy Trapeznekov, Yakov Butorin, and Karl Kort.

4

MARE ISLAND

Negotiations for repairs of the Russian vessels at the Mare Island Navy Yard had begun almost two years earlier, when the Russian vice consul at San Francisco, Petr Stepanovich Kostromitinov, wrote to the commandant of the shipyard, Cdr. David D. McDougal, requesting cost and conditions of docking.[1] McDougal had been relieved shortly afterward by Capt. William H. Gardiner in June of 1861. On May 28, 1862, Capt. Thomas O. Selfridge relieved Gardiner and would be in command during the time the Russian vessels were at the shipyard. Selfridge, a native of Massachusetts, had previously commanded the navy yard at Portsmouth, New Hampshire as well as the sloop *Dale* in the U.S. Pacific Squadron in the late 1840s. Earlier, he had also served onboard *North Carolina*, as a part of the Pacific Squadron, in the late 1830s. During the Mexican War Selfridge participated in the capture of *Matanzas* and *Guayams*, receiving a severe wound during the latter that effectively incapacitated him for future sea duty. A few months after taking command of the shipyard, he was promoted to the rank of commodore on July 16, 1862. The workforce at the Pacific coast's only shipyard with a large dry dock included 126 carpenters, 101 joiners, forty-one blacksmiths, forty-three machinists, eighteen painters, thirty-nine masons, eleven dockworkers, fourteen riggers, sixty-one laborers, and one sailmaker.[2]

Shortly after noon on Sunday, October 25, 1863, the first three Russian vessels arrived at Mare Island.

Commodore Thomas Selfridge, Commandant of Mare Island Naval Shipyard

They were the *Kalevala* under Captain Zheltukhin, the *Bogatyr* under Captain Chebyshev, and the *Gaidamak* under Captain Peshchurov.[3]

At the north end of San Francisco Bay, Mare Island measured five miles by two (1,066 acres). Its name had nothing to do with the Latin word for sea but rather with General Mariano Guadalupe Vallejo's horse, which fell off a raft one day while the general was transporting some of his belongings across the Carquinez Straits. He

Russian Squadron at Mare Island

was unable to rescue the mare at the time of the accident and gave her up for dead. Later, she was discovered grazing upon the island—hence the name Mare Island.

Upon their arrival at the island, the clipper ship *New Hampshire* was in the Pacific coast's only dry dock so they would each wait their turns to enter it. Dry-docking was extremely important because ships' hulls sometimes became so fouled that they dragged a lawn of sea grass six inches deep along with them, and this was the only way of scraping it off. In addition, the wooden hulls of ships had to be inspected for significant rotting.

❦

Not long after arriving at Mare Island, Admiral Popov gave a banquet onboard his flagship, the *Bogatyr*, for Admiral Bell, commander of the U.S. Pacific Squadron. Also present as invited guests were Capt. Joseph Lanman and other officers of the USS *Lancaster*; the commodore of the Spanish war-steamer; Captain Winder of Alcatraz; and Captain Scammon of the cutter *Shubrick*. Besides these, Gov. Leland Stanford and Congressman (and future governor) Frederick F. Low participated in the festivities. The *Alta California* described the banquet in glowing terms. "The dinner was a sumptuous one, and excellent taste was shown, both as regards the quality of the viands and the manner in which they were served, and also in the arrangement of the dishes, etc." The host occupied the head of the table. On his right sat Admiral Bell and on his left Governor

Stanford. The *Bogatyr's* band played various national airs and anthems of countries whose naval representatives were seated around the table. The *Alta California* concluded its description of the evening by stating, "The very best of feeling prevailed throughout, and the kindliest sentiments were interchanged between the officers of the three nations. At 11 o'clock the distinguished part separated, having enjoyed exceeding their international reunion in the floating home of the venerable Russian Admiral."[4]

The following day the commandant of the Mare Island Navy Yard notified the secretary of the navy that Admiral Popov and three vessels of his squadron had arrived for repairs and "the facilities of the yard have been extended to him."[5] That same day the second-class screw sloop USS *Narragansett* arrived. The 188-foot-long gunboat had been commissioned in 1859 and carried four thirty-two-pounders for armament.

On October 28 a fourth vessel in Admiral Popov's squadron arrived. The 1,070-ton Russian steam corvette *Abrek*, under the command of Captain Konstantin Pavlovich Pilkin, arrived in San Francisco, fifty-four days after sailing from Shanghai. The *Abrek* had been delayed in her arrival because of necessary repairs en route. She had departed Shankhaya in the Bering Sea with a weak mast and other problems, and had stopped at Sitka where Captain Pilkin selected and had a new mast made.[6] The *Abrek* carried six guns and 140 men, and had engines rated at three hundred horsepower.[7]

About the same time three Russian sailors were brought before U.S. Commissioner Chevers as deserters from the Russian fleet. The three men claimed that, when intoxicated, they had been put in a small room in a sailors' boarding house, near the waterfront, and confined there for two weeks. They said they did not want to desert, but wished to go back to the fleet.[8] Later investigation revealed that these Russian sailors had gone to the English consulate and signed articles of agreement and went immediately to the English vessel *Margaret Pugh*. They worked uncomplainingly onboard until the afternoon of the following day. Meanwhile, the $40 bounty, or two months advanced pay, was duly advanced by the captain of the *Margaret Pugh* to the boarding house keeper, or to the person who had induced the sailors to leave the service of the tsar.

On Saturday morning, October 31, the Russian sailors at Mare Island were startled by the fire alarm that sounded for the shipyard's pitch house, which was ablaze. The fire was discovered about 7:15 that morning and less than ten minutes later the alarm summoned the shipyard's firefighters. The fire was put out within about forty-five minutes, but not before it had destroyed the woodwork of the one-story brick building and a portion of its contents.[9] The following day, Sunday, about noon, the Russian steam corvette *Abrek* arrived at Mare Island from its previous anchorage in San Francisco.[10]

On Thursday, November 4, the *Gaidamak* became the first of Admiral Popov's vessels to enter floating dry dock at Mare Island.[11] The dry dock was a modified

Mare Island Naval Shipyard floating drydock

Vessel in Mare Island Naval Shipyard's
floating drydock

version of the sectional dry dock built at the Philadelphia shipyard. It was shipped in pieces from its
manufacturer in New York to Mare Island. The 325-
foot floating dry dock was actually composed of ten
sectional docks, each thirty-two feet wide and one hundred feet long, with six inches space between. To sink
the dry dock, gates were opened at each end of the main
tanks. As they filled with water the sections would
slowly sink. After all the sections had submerged, the
dock-master, who controlled the entire operation, signaled the *Gaidamak* to be floated into the now submerged dry dock. To raise the dock operators pumped
the water out of the sections and attempted to keep it
level with the floats. As the water was taken out the dry
dock would rise. To effect this, each section had three
pumps on each end, with a capacity to throw three hundred gallons a minute. They were connected to the machinery above by long rods that ran to the pumps on the
deck of the section.

When the vessel was centered, using centering
beams, the dock-master would then commence the raising of the dry dock by pumping water out of each tank.
As soon as the sections lightened a little, the floats were
started, and they moved downward on the great posts
just as fast as the posts rose. When the vessel was lifted
about twelve inches, the bilge blocks were run under to
support her all around. These were large oak blocks,
built up one on top of another and connected together
by iron dogs, so that they could be made high or low as
the shape of the vessel may require.[12]

Russian Steam Corvette *Rynda*

While the *Gaidamak* was in the dry dock the Russian steam corvette *Rynda* arrived in San Francisco harbor on the morning of November 7, thirty days after sailing from China. The *Rynda,* with the American flag flying from its foremast, fired a twenty-one gun national salute upon entering the harbor, which was answered by the guns on Fort Alcatraz and the frigate *Lancaster*. The smallest of the Russian Squadron, the *Rynda*, displacing just eight hundred tons, carried eleven guns and 160 men and was commanded by Captain Vladimor Grigorievich Basargin. The arrival of the *Rynda* completed the Russian fleet, which would spend the winter and spring in San Francisco.[13]

A few days later, on November 9, the *Gaidamack* was refloated and left the floating dry dock. The following morning the *Kalevala* entered floating dry dock at 11:30.

During the months that the Russians were at Mare Island they apparently made every effort to get their money's worth, because only a couple of weeks after they arrived, Commandant Selfridge sent naval constructor Melvin Simmons a note stating, "[I]n future, be pleased to inform me of any work the Russian men of war may require before it is commenced, as there is some work doing in the Construction Department which I never heard of until today, for these vessels."[14]

The Russians were very pleased with their experience at Mare Island. In a letter to his superiors in St. Petersburg, Admiral Popov commented on the "extraordinary kindness" (*chrezvychainaya predupredityclnost'*) they had received from the shipyard personnel. Besides making necessary repairs to the Russian vessels, the Americans had given the Russian sailors useful lessons in damage repair.[15]

The Mare Island officials also were pleased with the visit. Later, after all the repairs were completed and the Russian ships had gone to San Francisco, the shipyard commandant wrote to the secretary of the navy, stating that he was "pleased to add, that my intercourse with the Admiral and his officers, both official and social, have been most agreeable and harmonious."[16]

* * *

During their stay at Mare Island, two Russians frequently visited Captain Selfridge's quarters. Lieutenant Alexander Adolphovich Etolin and fifteen-year-old

Lieutenant Alexander Adolphovich Etolin

Midshipman Stepan O. Makarov, both of the *Bogatyr*, took English lessons from the captain's twenty-year-old daughter, Katherine. Lieutenant Etolin was born of a Finnish noble family in Russian America in 1841, the same year that the New Archangel Shipyard had launched the first steam vessel built in the Pacific. His father, Adolph Etolin, a native of Finland, had come to Russian America as a youth in the 1820s, becoming its governor in 1840. Lieutentant Etolin's early childhood would be spent in New Archangel (Sitka), a city of some thirteen hundred people at the time, many of them Finnish. He would move with his family to St. Petersburg in 1845, at the age of four.

**Katherine Selfridge, daughter of Mare Island
Naval Shipyard Commandant**

**Ned Selfridge, son of Mare Island
Naval Shipyard Commandant**

Both Russians, Etolin and Makarov, fell in love with their teacher. Makarov became jealous as he saw the relationship between Lieutenant Etolin and Miss Selfridge deepening. Makarov later described Etolin as "an intelligent, well educated gentleman, carpet-knight and excellent seaman." Makarov still loved Katherine many years later and wrote about his love for her in his diary. All the members of the Selfridge family were very friendly with the young midshipman. Because his own family situation was not very happy, he came to feel himself a member of the Selfridge family. He became very close friends with Katherine's younger brother "Ned" (Edward). Lieutenant Etolin would return to the United States six years later and marry his former teacher. The young midshipman became the famous Admiral Makarov, who was killed on the battleship *Petropavlovsk* during the Russo-Japanese war (1904–05). Makarov reportedly considered the months he spent in California as the happiest period in his life.[17] For many of the Russians, however, their time in San Francisco was not as happy. Far from home they suffered from homesickness and a desire to return to their homeland as soon as possible.[18]

Also during this time, another Russian officer, Captain Elfsberg, became friends with Captain Scammon of the *Shubrick*. Captain Elfsberg must have made a very favorable impression on the Revenue Cutter Service Captain because Scammon named his second son, born early in 1864, Alexander Elfsberg Scammon, and during his childhood called him Elfsberg.[19]

San Franciscans rejoiced on November 10 when the *Aquilla* arrived with a special cargo. Almost as soon as the Civil War had begun, the citizens and civic leaders of San Francisco expressed their desire for better harbor defenses than the unsinkable, but also immovable, army forts. They wanted a significant warship for the exclusive use of harbor defense. They believed that the cheapest and most expeditious solution was to have an ironclad steamer with a revolving gun tower. The previous February word had been received that the *Camanche*, an ironclad monitor, was being shipped to San Francisco for harbor defense duty.

The *Camanche*, a 1,875-ton Ericsson monitor, mounting two fifteen-inch guns, built by Secor Brothers, Jersey City, NJ, was disassembled and shipped to

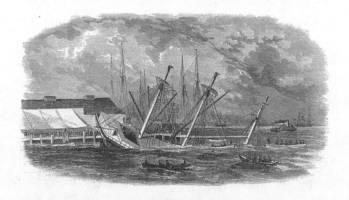

Wreck of the *Aquila* with the monitor *Camanche* on board

California on board *Aquilla*. Upon arrival it was to be assembled at Peter Donahue's Union Iron Works, recently established in the city. San Franciscans were rejoicing that at least they would have a significant warship defending their harbor and city. However, a few days after the *Aquilla's* arrival, on Sunday evening, November 14, a severe storm hit the city. Increasing in strength during the night, it became a howling gale by midnight. Wharfs were blown down and ships in the bay dragged their anchors. The *Aquilla*, as well as the parts for the *Camanche*, sank next to Hathaway's Wharf. San Franciscans were disheartened, for the *Aquila* had weathered hurricanes and eluded Confederate raiders in order to transport the long-sought monitor to their harbor, only to sink beside the pier. She would lie in the mud for a number of months before eventually being raised. By the time the *Camanche* was finally operational the need for harbor security had passed.

San Francisco's residents were also saddened when the USS *Lancaster* departed their harbor and sailed south to Central and South America. They had hoped the *Lancaster* would remain in the harbor until the USS *Saranac*, which was then undergoing repairs at Mare Island, could take her place. The *Saranac* was a 215-foot side-wheel steam sloop, commissioned in 1850 and assigned to the Pacific Squadron. One San Francisco newspaper lamented, "The little gunboat *Shubrick* and the steamer *Narragansett* are but poor adjuncts to the protection of the harbor compared to the frigate *Lancaster*."[20] The USS *Narragansett* was a 188-foot second-class screw sloop, commissioned in 1859.

On November 21 the *Rynda*, the last of the Russian vessels to arrive in San Francisco, arrived at Mare Island for repairs. About this same time, Rear Admiral Popov and his staff accepted an invitation to visit the Union Street public school. The admiral and his staff wore civilian clothes for their visit. The students sang national songs for the admiral; practiced calisthenic exercises; exhibited their proficiency in reading, arithmetic, and drawing; and generally illustrated the manner in which youth were trained to become American citizens. The admiral was "highly delighted" with the performances of the grammar and primary departments. He was especially impressed with the regular working order and system of the whole school. More than five hundred students were in attendance and sang the "Star Spangled Banner" and the "Red, White and Blue," demonstrating the patriotism of America's public school students.[21] The following month Admiral Popov and his staff visited the Mason Street School and were equally impressed with the scholastic proficiency displayed by the students.[22] On Tuesday of Thanksgiving week the *Kalevala* was refloated and departed the dry dock at Mare Island so that the shipyard workers would not have to work on America's first annual National Day of Thanksgiving on November 26. The custom house, mint, post office, and public places of business were closed, as were all the public schools. Many of the area churches held divine services, as did at least two Jewish synagogues. Bunting was displayed on public and private buildings and many of the vessels in the harbor were decorated with ensigns, pennants, and streamers.

Even though all the Russian vessels were at Mare Island, San Franciscans were again reminded of their presence when they had an opportunity to view a large portion of the equipment of the wrecked Russian steam corvette *Novick*, which was placed on display at the establishment of Mr. Charles Hare on Stewart Street on Saturday, November 28. Some five or six guns were on display. One was a twenty-four-pounder and the others were thirty-two-pounders. Also on display were a number of substantial and handsome copper chests, used as powder magazines. The engines had been saved, but not the boilers. The sails, made of "Russian duck" were also on display, in addition to various other articles.

On December 1 the *Gaidamak* departed Mare Island and anchored in the harbor off San Francisco. The Russian flagship *Bogatyr* would be in the Mare Island floating dry dock from December 2 to December 10 undergoing repairs. On the nineteenth the Russians were startled by a major earthquake that struck the bay area about 7:30 that evening. It was believed to have been the hardest shock felt in San Francisco since 1855 and was felt as far south as San Jose and Santa Clara. The *Bogatyr* would reenter the floating dry dock on December 31. The *Bogatyr* would depart the dry dock on January 2 and the *Abrek* entered it on the morning of January 5. During this time the commandant of the shipyard asked for rough estimates "of the probably expenditures" for material and labor "for the several vessels of the Russian Squadron"[23]

The same day that the *Bogatyr* reentered the dry dock, December 31, Secretary of the Navy Gideon Welles finally sent long-awaited instructions to Rear Admiral Bell regarding measures of protection for the city of San Francisco.

> SIR: Californians visiting the Department have expressed much anxiety with regard to the safety of that city [San Francisco] from sudden attack from sea, and for the purpose of allaying their fears and giving greater security to that important city the Department would be glad if you could so arrange your force as to keep one of your vessels constantly there. The *Wateree*, Commander F. K. Murray, will sail in the course of ten days or a fortnight to join your squadron, and it is contemplated to dispatch another steamer to you at an early day."[24]

From that time on, a U.S. Navy warship would almost always be present in San Francisco Harbor.

However, that was little consolation when the local newspapers reported on January 9 that the Confederate commerce raider *Alabama* was supposed to be on her way to the Pacific, "and naturally to San Francisco." Many San Franciscans would have felt more secure if the monitor *Camanche* was on patrol in the harbor, rather than lying in the mud at the bottom of the bay at the foot of Hathaway's Wharf. The paper went on to lament,

> There is no use disguising the fact that the guns mounted in our harbor are not what they should be; nor further, that we have no vessels of war, except the cockle shell *Shubrick*, at present in our harbor. Though she carried five guns "she does not amount to much."[25]

San Franciscans felt virtually defenseless from this possible threat because the *Saranac* was laid up at Mare Island. The *Lancaster* was at Guaymas and the *Narragansett* was cruising in the Gulf of Georgia.

In response to the fears of San Franciscans regarding the *Alabama,* Admiral Popov directed his flag officer, Captain Nakhinov, to offer the use of four complete sets of diving apparatus, with old and thoroughly experienced divers to work with them, and as many sailors for the fleet as could be used to advantage in raising the *Aquila* and recovering the *Camanche*. Admiral Popov also suggested a plan for raising the vessel by attaching a large number of wrought iron straps to her sides and by driving bolts into her hull above and below the waterline, and as near the keel as possible. Then, he recommended, attach a purchase to these, and lift her bows sufficiently to get chains under her, and permit her cargo, the *Camanche*, to be removed. This was considered a very generous offer by the Russians, and would have been accepted if the divers and diving apparatus ordered from New York by the underwriters had not arrived on the next steamer from Panama.[26]

Many San Franciscans complained about the apparent indifference of the insurance underwriters to their plight. San Franciscans believed that skilled divers existed in the city that could have begun efforts long before the divers and equipment arrived from New York. When those divers and equipment did finally arrive, all attempts by the divers failed to raise the vessel. However, these divers managed to salvage all the missing parts. With these salvaged parts from *Aquila's* hulk, *Camanche* would finally be launched on November 14, 1864, but not commissioned until August 22, 1865. The vessel was never used for the defense of San Francisco. Laid up at Mare Island throughout most of her career, *Camanche* served as a training ship for the California Naval Militia in 1896 and 1897. She was sold at Mare Island on March 22, 1899.

The Russians became enamored with the U.S. Navy's monitors that they first observed during the war. Construction of ten monitors based on John Ericsson's design was begun in Russia in 1863 and completed three years later.

During the winter of 1863–64 rumors circulated that not only the Confederate cruiser *Sumter* was off the California coast, but also the Confederate cruiser *Alabama,* and one or both were planning to attack the unguarded city. Excited citizens appealed to Admiral Popov for protection. In view of this fear of attack Admiral Popov, without consulting with his superiors, gave orders to his officers that should an enemy ship come into the harbor, the ranking officer should at once give signal "to put on steam for clear action." At the same time a Russian officer would warn the vessel that the squadron would assist the local authorities in repelling any attack. If this warning was ignored and the vessel opened fire, then the squadron was to open fire.[27]

When St. Petersburg learned of Popov's order his superiors were not pleased. Gokrtchakov urged Popov to observe the strictest neutrality. Ambassador Stoeckl sent Popov the following guidance:

> From all the information to be obtained here it would seem that the Confederate cruisers aim to operate only in the open sea and it is not expected that cities will be attacked and San Francisco is in no danger. What the corsairs do in the open sea does not concern us; even if they fire on the forts, it is your duty to be strictly neutral. But in the case the corsair passes the forts and threatens the city, you have then the right, in the name of humanity, and not for political reasons, to prevent this misfortune. It is to be hoped that the naval strength at your command will bring about the desired result and that you will not be obliged to use force and involve our government in a situation which it is trying to keep out of.

The rumors concerning the *Alabama* and *Sumter* proved to be false. The Confederate cruisers did not appear and the attack on San Francisco never took place. It never became necessary for the tsar's Pacific Squadron to execute Admiral Popov's orders, which would have made Russia an active ally of the United States in the Civil War. However, rumors persisted that a Confederate privateer was being fitted out at Victoria, Vancouver Island. The *Narragansett* sailed from San Francisco on December 11, 1863, for Victoria to investigate and find out if the rumors were true.

Throughout January all five Russian vessels continued to undergo repairs at Mare Island. When not undergoing repairs the Russian vessels would anchor off Saucelito. In early February Admiral Popov held a reception for Commodore Selfridge aboard the *Rynda*. Admiral Popov came down from Mare Island on the *Rynda* and anchored off the Pacific street wharf. Upon Commodore Selfridge's arrival on board, the *Rynda* fired a thirteen-gun salute and ran up the American flag. The *Rynda*, getting up steam, ran back to Mare Island with the two commodores on board.

On February 11 the USS *Narragansett*, now under the command of Cdr. Selim E. Woodworth, returned from Puget Sound. A 1,235-ton screw corvette, the *Narragansett* had been launched in 1859 and carried one eleven-inch gun and four thirty-two-pound guns. However, her presence was of little comfort when on February 13 the *Alta California* reported that six vessels had been built in England for the Emperor of

China, but due to a disagreement over the original contract when the vessels arrived in China, they had been sold to the Confederacy and that "together with the *Alabama*, which we know to be in Chinese waters, are intended for an attack upon San Francisco."

That same Saturday, at about six o'clock in the evening, Captain Zheltukhin, commanding officer of the *Kalevala*, while out riding with a lady on the Ocean House road, just back of the Mission Dolores, was seriously injured in a carriage accident. Dr. De Castro, who had been with the party at the Ocean House, came past the scene of the accident without noticing anything unusual. However, on arriving at the Nightingale House, the doctor saw the captain's horses running down the street without a buggy, and immediately drove back to see what had occurred. At the foot of the first hill back of the mission, on the Ocean House Road, he found the captain, lying unconscious by the roadside and his lady companion weeping over him, supposing him to be dead. The buggy had been upset at the sharp turn of the road, and the captain was thrown from the buggy, smashing his head against a rock with such force as to fracture his skull at the right temple, and to smash the whole upper part of the right side of his face. The doctor transported the captain to the Nightingale where he still remained unconscious. His lady companion was sent home in a carriage. Dr. Twitchell was called in, to render such surgical assistance as was possible. Dr. De

Castro went immediately into the city and summoned the Russian consul and a Russian physician, who accompanied him out to the Nightingale. After consulting with Dr. Twitchell the Russian physician had the captain moved to Dr. Zeile's hospital on Pacific Street. The injured captain had recently applied to the Imperial Government for permission to return to Russia, and had been daily expecting the summons to return to his home beyond the sea. The horses were taken down to the Omnibus Railroad Company's depot on Howard Street, and the broken carriage was left at the Abbey Hotel where its owner could recover it.[28]

Captain Zheltukhin began to regain consciousness at two o'clock the following afternoon, and by ten o'clock that evening was able to articulate some words clearly enough to be understood. Many rejoiced because this indicated that his injuries were probably not fatal and that he would recover![29]

A few days later it was reported that Captain Zheltukhin still remained in the hospital and was unable to speak distinctly due to an injury of his jaw, which also made it difficult for him to take any nourishment. Nevertheless, "it is thought that there is now no doubt of his ultimate recovery."[30] By early March he reportedly was making steady progress and was able to walk about his rooms daily. He also had partially recovered his speech.[31]

With Captain Zheltukhim disabled, the corvette *Kalevala* was placed under the command of Lieutenant

Gerkin. To give Lieutenant Gerkin a chance to acquaint himself with his new ship, Admiral Popov sent the *Kalevala* to sea for a five day cruise.

Somewhat surprisingly, in the midst of fear of the rumored Anglo-Chinese pirate fleet, together with the *Alabama,* the *Alta California* opined on February 15, that while coastal commerce would be utterly paralyzed upon the arrival of such a fleet, the city could be defended by the *Narragansett* and *Shubrick*, currently in the port, together with other USN ships in the Pacific who could be sent there.[32]

Yet, two days later it opined "that every attempt made during the last two years to place this city and State in a proper condition of defense has failed." The article went on to criticize the state legislature for its failure to appropriate any funds for arms and munitions, or procuring a steamer and covering her with iron— after the style of the *Merrimac* (CSS *Virginia*), for the defense of the harbor. It also stated that Washington had responded by sending the *Camanche,* but it still was underwater. The article concluded by criticizing the legislature for its failure to provide funds for San Francisco to erect batteries at certain points in the harbor.[33]

A few days after that an editorial again addressed the fear of "a suspicious fleet in Chinese waters" and urged San Franciscans to take matters into their own hands by mounting older forty-two-pound guns at Fort Point, at Black Point, and on Angel Island and man these guns with state militia. It also urged that an effort be made to induce the Navy Department to keep in the harbor vessels of war that were currently there, and to inform Commodore Bell, at Acapulco, of the rumors then in circulation.[34]

A few days later, another editorial acknowledged that the city was not without defense. It had Fort Point and Alcatraz as well as the *Shubrick* and *Narragansett*, the *Monitor,* and the *Saranac*. However, it urged that the city's defenses could be greatly increased. It urged the recovery of the two fifteen-inch guns from the *Camanche* for use against the *Alabama*.

On the morning of February 16, the Russian flagship *Bogatyr* exchanged salutes with the shipyard and steamed to San Francisco. On the twenty-first the *Abrek* also departed Mare Island. On February 22 all five ships of Russia's Pacific Squadron would be in the San Francisco harbor to participate in one of America's biggest celebrations, Washington's birthday. Admiral Popov, ever sensitive to international courtesy, took the precaution of inquiring from the local U.S. Navy officers how far it would be acceptable for him to join in the celebration of the day, suggesting that he would like to join to the fullest extent possible, with the means at his command.

The batteries at Fort Point and Alcatraz, and the artillery companies in the city fired salutes at sunrise in honor of the holiday. U.S. Navy vessels and the *Shubrick* each fired twenty-one gun salutes at noon. The Stars and Stripes flew from almost every place of business and place of residence. The American and some of the foreign shipping in the harbor were decked with bunting. The news reports made special commendation of the Russian ships.

> Conspicuous among the vessels thus adorned was the flag-ship of the Russian squadron under Admiral Popoff [*sic*], which was superbly decorated with flags, a line of them running over the whole vessels from stem to stern, with the Stars and Stripes conspicuously at the head, and at 12 [noon] a full National salute was fired from her heavy batteries, the guns being worked with such rapidity that the whole steamer was in a few seconds enveloped in a dense cloud of smoke, through which only the flashes of the cannon could be seen by the observers on shore."[35]

A few days later that same paper wrote, "Our citizens cannot but appreciate this demonstration by the Admiral on behalf of the nation he represents."[36]

The day after the celebration, Admiral Popov gave a grand dinner aboard his flagship, the *Bogatyr,* as an expression of appreciation for the recent Russian Ball. A number of citizens, officers, and civilians, most of whom were connected with the Russian Ball, were invited. About twenty-five persons were present. The steamer's boats conveyed the guests on board. A table was spread in the admiral's saloon. Following the meal the admiral was very happy and appreciative in his remarks. A local paper described those remarks by saying that,

> in a neat little speech, [the admiral] complimented the American nation, and expressed the warm friendship of his people towards our country. He reviewed the rise of each nation, and the points of similitude and of common interest which have ever tended to unite them in bonds of friendship and amity. After reciting many points of Russian history, he closed with the last great acts of the two Governments—the emancipation of serfs in Russia and slaves in America.

The dinner was enlivened by music from the band, after which the guests enjoyed a beautiful moonlight row to the landing.[37]

About a week later, on March 2, Admiral Popov and his fellow Russians celebrated the anniversary of the coronation of Emperor Alexander II and Russian serf emancipation. The Russian flagship *Bogatyr* and the Russian merchant vessels *Abo* and *Caesarvich* were gaily decked with flags. The *Bogatyr* fired a national salute of twenty-one guns at noon. The *Shubrick* and a number of American merchant vessels in port were also decorated with flags in honor of the occasion, and the Shubrick responded to the Bogatyr's salute.[38] Admiral Popov gave a grand reception onboard the Bogatyr to the foreign consuls and military, naval, and civil officers of the United States and the state of California.

Two days after this joyful celebration the Russians undoubtedly witnessed the outpouring of grief over the death of the Reverend Thomas Starr King on March 4. The Unitarian minister had only resided in the city since 1860 but during the four years before his premature death, at age forty, from diphtheria, he quickly had become popular as both a preacher and a person. As many as forty thousand persons had come to hear him at mass meetings where his eloquent talks for the U.S. Sanitary Commission tremendously aided support of the Union Army and helped influence California to the Union side. King's eloquence was so great that his supporters said of him, "King saved California for the Union." Businesses and government offices would close in mourning for several days.

The day after Thomas Starr King's death the Russians, anchored in the harbor, experienced the largest earthquake yet to strike San Francisco since Americans settled in the bay. It occurred at eleven minutes before nine o'clock in the morning. The shaking reportedly continued for almost a full minute. Heavy swells rolled in from the bay and broke under the wharves with considerable force. Riding at anchor, their ships rolled with the heavy swells. They perhaps could see from their ships, or maybe later, while ashore, that the walls of quite a number of buildings cracked and plastering in many places was broken, and in some instances glass windows broke.[39]

The outpouring of grief at the funeral of Thomas Starr King on March 6 no doubt moved the Russians. Business and schools were closed and a huge crowd came to pay their respects. The masons and military participated in the service, which the governor and principal federal and state officials attended. The Russians were probably touched that this California martyred hero was laid to rest in the same cemetery as one of their own, the Lone Hill Cemetery. However, a few months after the Russian squadron departed, the remains of Thomas Starr King were removed to a sarcophagus in the front of the Unitarian Church.

A week and a half later, the Russians experienced a rare, but very heavy hailstorm that left San Francisco's streets covered to the depth of an inch or more. A thunder shower at mid-day had deluged the city streets with water and then changed to hail. The hail permitted the city's residents, and perhaps some of the Russians, to indulge themselves in a rare event in San Francisco—a snowball fight.

On March 7 Admiral Popov gave a dinner aboard his flagship, the *Bogatyr*. It was purely a social gathering for the friends he had made in the city. The vessel's band played musical selections throughout the dinner. It was later reported that Annis Merrill, an enthusiastic abolitionist, was among the guests and that at the dinner he leaned over to Admiral Popov and asked, "Admiral, suppose a fleet of Rebel privateers should suddenly appear off the Golden Gate and threaten to lay this city in ruins. What would you do?" The admiral reportedly replied, "I would not only lend you my guns, I would lend you my ships, I would lend you my men, I would give you my ammunition and the chances are I would go along myself."[40]

⟡

Despite his warm reception and excellent treatment, Admiral Popov found his time in San Francisco somewhat frustrating. Early in 1864 the Mare Island Navy Yard increased its charge by fifteen percent for dry-docking commercial and foreign vessels. Popov's vessel, the *Rynda*, was the first ship to have the pay the new, higher price.[41] In addition, the resources of the shipyard were limited and many objects like machine parts were required to be made by local manufacturers. Some carpenters received $5.50 per day. Bargains were hard to find. This greatly increased the admiral's costs. On at least one occasion he wrote to his superiors in St. Petersburg asking for an increase in funding. In addition he found the San Francisco Bay area to be a very expensive place to be for his officers and crew. He reported that his officers often paid from two to three dollars for a trip from Mare Island to San Francisco, but sometimes paid even more, once up to $10 for this one-way trip. Because of these high personal expenses he had allocated a daily allowance of $10 for commanders, but only $5 for other officers. Even this, sometimes, was insufficient. He offered as example the case of Lieutenant Nakhimov, his chief financial and supply officer.

Because Lieutenant Nakhimov was constantly in San Francisco seeking supplies, he had to keep an apartment in San Francisco. Admiral Popov had increased Nahimov's daily allowance to that of commanders, $10 a day, but even that proved inadequate. Admiral Popov pleaded with the Russian admiralty to distribute to him, by Crown authority, 1,200 Russian rubles to cover his expenses. Popov also had to order a considerable amount of a particular type of blue woolen cloth for use in manufacturing uniforms for his officers and crews.[42]

In addition, Popov complained to the admiralty that he had been directed to send any superfluous officers of his squadron to the Atlantic Squadron, sending them via Panama in one of his ships. Popov had decided to transfer Lieutenant Burachka and Engineer-Mechanic Sub-Lieutenant Prograsky to the Atlantic Squadron. However, he reminded the admiralty that a cruise to Panama and back using either a clipper or one of his squadron as the ship would be far from cheap, and would further increase his expenses.

In a letter to his superiors in St. Petersburg, Admiral Popov again complained about the extraordinary expenses they had incurred in San Francisco. For coal he had to pay more than $30 per ton, buying it in coin, not in bank notes. He noted that the Mare Island authorities were still doing their final calculations, but it appeared that over the six months the vessels were at the shipyard that they had to pay over $80 per ton on occasion. Popov also noted the individual expenses of his officers. They had to pay $4 to have their boots cleaned. To wash a dozen whites, stockings, and handkerchiefs, it cost $1.50–$2. Big sheets cost $3 apiece for laundering. He reported that with those prices it was not surprising that all his officers were in debt.[43]

By early March, Admiral Popov considered his squadron in complete readiness and wanted to take it to sea for a brief, post-shipyard, "shakedown" cruise for a few days, and for artillery practice. Before getting underway, Admiral Popov left his supply officer, Lieutenant Nakhimov, in San Francisco with full authority to act for him. The squadron weighed anchor at noon on March 20 and sailed out the Golden Gate. The *Bogatyr* fired a salute of twenty-one guns when it passed the *Shubrick* and Fort Point, but since it was Sunday, the salute was not returned. While the Russians were at sea, the vessels encountered very strong winds and high seas. While the cannons operated to the admiral's expectation, the *Gaidamak* sprung its rigging masts and later need repairs. When the Russian squadron returned from its brief training cruise on March 25, the *Gaidamak* proceeded to Mare Island to receive a new mast, and for other repairs. Since the Russian's salute had not be returned when she departed the harbor, because it had been a Sunday, Fort Point and the *Shubrick* had arranged to fire a twenty-one gun salute from the fort and from the *Shubrick* on Admiral Popov's return. The *Gaidamak* sailed from Mare Island on April 8, bringing to an end the Russian squadron's time at the shipyard.

5

THE RUSSIAN BALL

Almost as soon as San Franciscans learned that wealthy New Yorkers had held a grand ball at the Astor House on November 5, in honor of Russians visiting their port, they began planning a ball for the Russian officers who were visiting their port. The organizers decided to hold it on Tuesday evening, November 17, in Union Hall on the south side of Howard Street, between Third and Fourth Streets. They hoped that this ball would be public evidence of the friendly feeling that existed between the government of the tsar and the citizens of the United States. It was announced that invitations would be sent for this "Russian Ball," and that it would be a subscription ball, the expenses of which would be paid by a few wealthy citizens. Therefore, all invitations were entirely gratuitous to such persons as received them.

The notes of invitation were engraved with the letters "U.S." at the top, with the letter "R" interwoven

between them, printed in a darker color and surrounded
by a wreath of oak and laurel. The invitation stated:

> The Citizens of San Francisco desiring to
> give expression to the feelings of amity and
> respect which they entertain toward Russia
> as a Nation respectfully tender Admiral A.
> A. Popoff [*sic*] and Officers of H.I.R.M.
> Squadron, a Complimentary Ball, to be given
> at the Union Hall, on Tuesday evening, No-
> vember 17th, 1863. You are cordially invited.

The invitations, of which twenty-four hundred
were issued, included this engraved ticket:

> *U.R.S. Complimentary Ball to Admiral Popoff*
> [*sic*] *and Officers of H.I.R.M. Squadron.*
> At Union Hall, Tuesday Evening, Nov. 17th,
> 1863.
> Mr. _____ _____.
> *Dancing to commence at 9 ½ o'clock.*

The committee in charge of arrangements included
Governor-Elect Frederick F. Low (Gov. Leland Stanford
was not a resident of San Francisco, but Mr. Low had
been residing in the city for some months and represented
the civil authority of the state); Rear Adm. Charles H.
Bell, commander of the U.S. Pacific Squadron; Brig. Gen.
George Wright, commander of the Department of the
Pacific; the honorable Charles James, collector of the

port (the highest federal official of the executive department on the Pacific Coast); and the honorable H. P. Coon, mayor of San Francisco.

The *Alta California* reported that those who failed to receive invitations were not chagrined, but rather that they "rejoiced that our Muscovite visitors had so superb entertainment given them." The writer went on to say that this entertainment was given not only out of compliment to the city's Russian visitors, but also for the purpose of strengthening the bonds between the United States and Russia.[1]

*　　　　　*

The *Rynda* left her anchorage off San Francisco at nine o'clock in the morning on the day of the ball, after taking on board a committee of citizens to escort Admiral Popov and thirty-five officers of the Russian fleet from Mare Island to the city for the event. The *Rynda* arrived at Mare Island at noon, where Admiral Popov and his officers boarded, and the party departed at 1:45 p.m. for San Francisco. The *Rynda* speedily got underway, accompanied by the *Shubrick*, and she ran down below Angel Island, and then over toward Alcatraz. Because of Captain Winder's absence, no salute was given to this fortification beyond the dipping of the flag. Most of the ships in the harbor flew bunting at the mastheads in honor of the Russians. Just at dusk, the *Lancaster*'s heavy guns thundered forth a salute of thirteen guns to Admiral Popov. Almost immediately the *Shubrick* also fired a salute.

The *Rynda* duly responded to the salutes with her cannons. Unfortunately, while returning the salutes of the American vessels in the harbor, a cannon prematurely discharged. One Russian sailor was killed and blown overboard by the explosion and another sailor was injured. The *Rynda* immediately lowered a boat, but rescuers were unable to recover the remains of the man who went overboard. The injured sailor's arm was shattered; he received prompt surgical aid and later recovered.

On December 4 the remains of a middle-aged man were found floating in the bay off Clark's Point. The body was taken to the "dead-house" (morgue), where it was later identified as that of the Russian sailor who had been killed. His Russian sailor's clothing made it easy to identify him, as well as a sailor's jack-knife that was fastened to his body with a lanyard and the fact that a part of one arm had been blown away. By order of the commanding officer of the *Rynda*, his remains were buried at Lone Mountain Cemetery in San Francisco. Established in 1854, the cemetery was three miles from the city plaza and had a view of both the Pacific Ocean and San Francisco Bay. Its name was changed to Laurel Hill Cemetery in 1867.

As the *Rynda* steamed up toward the Broadway Wharf (between Battery and Front Streets), the reception committee, consisting of Mr. James, customs collector; Mr. W. B. Farwell; and a naval officer, left the Pacific Wharf steps in the custom house barge and were rowed to the *Rynda*. Here, Admiral Popov courteously received them. After the admiral disembarked at the wharf, a flag was hoisted as the signal for the grand national salute, to be fired by Bluxome's Battery. A few minutes later, other officers of the fleet landed from other boats and a large number of carriages were waiting at the wharf to carry the admiral and his officers to Union Hall.

Thousands of San Francisco's citizens had congregated, waiting for hours for the arrival of "their Muscovite brethren of the Old World." The wharfs and vessels and sheds in the immediate vicinity of the Pacific Wharf were crowded with these men, women, and children. They broke forth into a loud ovation when the Russian officers finally arrived, wearing gold-laced chapeaux.[2] Many San Franciscans noticed that the Russian officers had twice the gold lace and buttons on their uniforms than that of the American officers.[3] Captain Scammon of the *Shubrick* and all of the U.S. Navy officers in attendance were in full dress uniforms, with gold epaulets replacing their normal shoulder straps; they all were wearing regulation swords.

Those officials in attendance included officers from Benicia Barracks, Forts Point and Alcatraz, and the Mare Island Navy Yard. Gov. Leland Stanford and the consuls from England, Sweden, France, Belgium, and Russia were also present.

At about 9:30 p.m. the distinguished guests of the evening—Admiral Popov and the officers of his squadron—arrived. Bell and his officers, as well as General Wright and his staff, received Admiral Popov at the upper end of the ballroom. The Russian navy officers and the American army and navy officers shook hands and made desperate attempts to pronounce each other's names.

Admiral Popov gave a brief greeting in English and the ball was opened. Dancing commenced, and guests continued to pour in until midnight. Music for the ball was provided by forty musicians, divided into two bands—one group of fifteen to perform during the intervals of dancing and the other group of twenty-five to furnish the dance music.

Union Hall was located over the Omnibus Railroad Company's depot on Howard Street. As the largest finished public hall on the Pacific Coast, it had but one or two superiors in size and elegance in the entire United States. It was gorgeously decorated for the ball. In the center of the stage, on which the orchestra was seated, were columns supporting arches that bore the Imperial Arms of Russia and around which floated the U.S. flag. On either side of the stage were two large allegorical pictures—the one on the right was emblematic of the horrible word "disunion"; the one on the left represented Unity and Love. At the base of the latter were real specimens of peace and prosperity in the shape of corn, sheaves of wheat, parcels of fruit and flowers, a dismounted cannon encircled by a wreath, and the implements of husbandry. At the base of the stage was a picture of the Eureka Bear, painted on a semicircle, and on top of which were arms radiated. This stood out in bold relief from the national flags of Russia and the United States, which were displayed behind and across the entire extent of the stage.

On both sides of the large hall eighteen pillars and arches were erected and covered with evergreens. Little cages with warbling canaries were suspended from the center of each arch, which were also surmounted by the shields and flags of Russia and the United States. In the central arches on both sides of the hall were portraits of the emperor and empress of Russia. At the extreme end of the hall and in front of the gallery there was a picture of President George Washington, bearing the inscription "The Father of Our Country," supported by two angels. The space between the arches and side walls of the hall was eight feet and suited admirably for the purpose of a promenade during the dancing and the intervals between, although the hall was somewhat crowded.

The panels on the walls were decorated with flags, wreaths, and mottoes that reflected the sentiments of the citizens of San Francisco. These included the following: "Russia and the United States—friends in peace and war." "*Non sibi sed omnibus*" (Not yourself, but everyone). "*Cor unum, via una*" (One heart, one path). "The First Alexander advocated our peace in 1812, the second Alexander prevents war in 1863." "The world has learned lessons of liberty from the Czar of Russia."

"Liberty, the radiant jewel in the Imperial crown of Russia." "The Union now and forever." Wine was more plentiful than water. The committee had also purchased every bottle of champagne available in the city, which would not have been enough. However, a potential crisis was averted by the timely arrival of the ship *Fabius*, from France, which was filled with champagne that had been ordered expressly for the occasion.

The supper room was thrown open at eleven o'clock and kept open until four the following morning. The menu, printed in gold on a broad band of white satin, listed under the heading of "Appetizers" such items as: "Oysters, raw or pickled; Terrapins au vin Madere; Boned Turkey; Truffles; Boiled Westphalia Ham in Champagne and ornamented; Vollauvent a la Financiere, [and] Smoked Tongue, iced and jellied." Next came six salads, followed by the roast game, the latter including "Turkey, Duck, Pigeons, Bacassin, Chicken, Goose, Quail, Snipe, &c., &c." Under the term "Confectionary," numerous delicacies were listed, among them "Charlotte de Russe; Jelly au Marosquin; Marenques au Confiture; Jelly au Rum, and All Kinds of Fruit." Five varieties of ice cream followed and then came what may have been the highlight of the evening for all those in attendance—a series of "masterpieces of the pastry-cook's art" called "Pyramids." One bore the title "Temple, with American and Russian flags"; another was "Russian Man-of-War"; and a third, "Kremlin of Moscow." The menu listed two final categories: "Cakes and Fruits." Sixteen varieties of cake were offered.

The supper room walls were decorated and emblazoned with every conceivable color of flag. Every state in the Union was represented by its flag and motto. On one side of the room was a fountain, which sent forth streams that glistened in the gaslight. After eating, the guests returned to the hall and danced until daylight.

Before the ball even commenced, the committee specified that it should end at four o'clock the following morning. The moment that hour arrived, the orchestra stopped playing, to the not small disappointment of many who seemed anxious to continue dancing until dawn. By five o'clock the hall was almost empty, thus ending an incident in San Francisco's history that many hoped "posterity will not willingly let die."

As the grand ball ended, however, a problem arose. After the orchestra stopped playing, a huge throng of guests—including Admiral Popov, Governor Stanford, General Allen, and Admiral Bell—were all waiting in line for their hats. All the hats and coats had to be passed out of a little square hole by two attendants. Under pressure from the impatient departing guests, the attendants had difficulty finding the right hats for the right heads. The guests finally became so impatient with the increasing wait that they eventually forced the door of the cloakroom open. At that point the two attendants fled. As the rush of guests entered the cloakroom, they immediately began looking through all the hats for their own. "I want my hat," said one. "Take a better one than your own," said another, "and be content." Many, seeing the confusion, decided to just take a hat and hoped to straighten everything out later.[4]

Among the articles lost were a Russian chapeau, a Russian sword, a U.S. Navy sword, and the Mexican consul's cloth talma (cape), lined with velvet and silk. Gentlemen who lost any of these articles were advised to call at the committee rooms, No. 3 Pioneer Building.[5]

Admiral Popov reportedly "emerged with the heavy saber of a cavalry officer, instead of his own gilt-scabbarded delicate blade, and in the place of his own plumed champeau, an undress fireman's cap lettered 'Eureka No.5.'"[6] In the days following the banquet, the streets of San Francisco saw a variety of new faces, or rather heads. Some, who before the banquet had worn black "stove pipes," were seen wearing white "wide awakes" (low-crowned, soft felt hats). Some discovered that the fine overcoats they had just purchased for the banquet were nowhere to be seen. But not withstanding this mix-up of hats and coats, everyone seemed to have enjoyed themselves and looked upon the whole situation with a sense of humor.

The entire cost of the ball was estimated to be between $14,000 and $16,000. The entertainment cost about $10,000 and the decorations for the ball were contracted for $1,000. Many San Franciscans thought it was money well spent. They believed it to be a guarantee of the good feeling existing between Russia and the United States. In reflecting upon the ball, one San Francisco newspaper stated:

> We have had our Russian ball here, and in New York and Boston the Russians have been feted to repletion. It is a good job done up; it is an excellent thing to have accomplished so neatly. So hereafter it is to be understood that Russia is America's bosom friend and America Russia's. They occupy different platforms, they have slightly differing styles of civilization. Religiously they look at the same cross from somewhat different standpoints. Politically they widely disagree—one is a republic, the other a monarchy. Their languages are a mutual puzzle—the Russian is slow to learn ours, and we can never speak theirs if we know it, ever so well. Her eagle has two heads, ours naturally but one. Her head is the Czar, ours the people. Yet with all these bars between us there is one strong impulse affecting both jointly. . . . Both are busy unshackling their slaves, both are repenting of an old sin, and both aim at freedom of the people. . . . Cheers for Russia! The shaggy-coated stranger of the northern wilds

proved a friend in a region where we scarcely thought of looking for one. May the harmony between the nations be perpetual.[7]

Another San Francisco paper reported the following: "A lady who was present at the ball given in New York to the Prince of Wales—and that was one of the finest balls ever given in the great Eastern metropolis—says that it was inferior in the style of decoration, and in the dresses of the ladies, to the Russian Ball of San Francisco."[8]

Not everyone, however, was thrilled with the ball. Those who championed the lower classes criticized it for only including the city's elite. "The Russian ball, by the way, is still a standing joke with us. The Negro minstrels burlesque it every night. People are as much ashamed now to confess that they were at it as they were before proud of boasting that they had tickets to it. So wags the world. Vive the Snobocracy!"[9]

The Russian Ball provided San Franciscans with the opportunity not only to honor their Russian visitors, but also to formally and socially express their appreciation for all they had done for the city. It also provided an opportunity to express the great friendship between tsarist Russia and the United States, two nations that indeed were both "friends in peace and war."

6

FINAL DAYS

May and June of 1864 brought little good news from the Civil War in the east. The Battle of the Wilderness on May 5 and 6 was a tactical defeat for Gen. Ulysses S. Grant, who had suffered eighteen thousand casualties. A few days later, at the Battle of Spotsylvania Court House, Grant was again unable to defeat Gen. Robert E. Lee's Army of Northern Virginia. Then in early June, Grant's attack had been repulsed at the Battle of Cold Harbor, with twelve thousand Union troops killed or wounded.

However, by that time the European war clouds had passed away. Russia had held firm and won. Great Britain was willing to call names but not to fight, and France was helpless without Great Britain. France offered to compromise and eventually even to aid Russia in quelling the Polish revolt. Gradually the insurrection in Poland was put down and the threat of a European war subsided. Admiral Popov and his officers believed that their coming to the United States was, if not altogether, at least in a very great measure, responsible for England's change of heart, and consequently for the prevention of the war.[1] It was, of course, for various reasons that England decided to remain neutral on the Polish question, but the presence of the Russian cruisers both in the Atlantic and Pacific ports of the United States undoubtedly played a major part in influencing British statesmen to adopt that policy.

On April 26, 1864, Prince Gortchakov, the Russian minister of foreign affairs, told General-Adjutant Krabbe—who directed the Russian navy while Grand Duke Constantine, general-admiral of the navy, was in Warsaw—that the emperor said there was no longer any need for the fleet to remain in the United States. Orders were dispatched to Admiral Popov at San Francisco the following day.

About that same time Admiral Popov received a telegram from Admiral Lesovskii of the Atlantic Squadron that notified him of the Russian admiralty's order to promptly dispatch the corvette *Rynda* and the clipper *Gaidamak* to join the Atlantic Squadron in New York. Earlier Popov had been advised that in case of a peaceful solution to the Polish crisis, the *Rynda* and *Gaidamak* were to be sent to Kronstadt. Popov had delayed sending two ships because of this apparent conflict. Within a few weeks his earlier orders were confirmed and he would indeed send them to Kronstadt.

On the eve of Orthodox Easter that spring, Admiral Popov invited several local Orthodox Christians, including Russians and Serbs, to attend an Easter Vigil

Liturgy aboard his flagship, the *Bogatyr*. Father Kirill, a Hieromonk from the Tikhvin First Class Monastery and the admiral's chaplain, presided at the service. After that service Admiral Popov came up with the idea of establishing an Orthodox Society in San Francisco. An organizational meeting was held a few weeks later at the halls of the city, with fifteen charter members who each contributed $20.00 in gold. By the end of 1864 the newly established Orthodox Society in San Francisco, which included Serbs, Russians, and Greeks, had $428.38 in a San Francisco Savings Union Bank. From this beginning would come the first Orthodox church in California.[2]

Admiral Popov and his staff undoubtedly had greeted Prince Dimitrii Petrovich Maksutov, newly appointed governor of Russian America when he arrived in San Francisco with his family on May 7, aboard the *China*. The prince, a widower, had married Maria Vladimirovna Aleksandrovich, the nineteen-year-old daughter of a former governor of Irkutsk, a few months earlier on January 22. He and his new bride, along with his two oldest children by his first wife, had departed St. Petersburg on February 7 en route to Liverpool. Upon their arrival in New York they had taken the Panama route to San Francisco. Maksutov had previously been the assistant governor of the Russian American colony. Born into one of the oldest noble families of Russia, he was one of the Russian navy's best men, having distinguished himself during the Crimean War at the Battle of Petropavlovsk. Of his many decorations he wore only one, the white cross of St. George, which he had been awarded for bravery at Petropavlovsk. Because he was a captain in rank, Prince Maksutov was known by Admiral Popov and many of his officers knew Prince Maksutov. There had been rumors that Russian America might be sold, but the president of the Imperial Council had recently pledged to give the Russian-America Company another twenty-year charter. To reassure the residents of the colony that it had a stable future, the prince brought his family with him.

On May 14 the prince, together with his new bride and his young daughters, Anna, age four, and Elena, almost three, both by his deceased wife, Adelaide, embarked onboard the admiral's flagship, the *Bogatyr*, en route to New Archangel. According to a popular legend the prince also brought on board with him a Rugosa, or Turkestan rose, to be planted on the grave of his first wife, buried at New Archangel, already commonly referred to as Sitka. That rose would become known as the Sitka Rose.

On the way, the *Bogatyr* visited Victoria on Vancouver Island, the capital of the crown colony of British Columbia, from May 6–9, probably to take on coal. The ship then steamed out the Strait of Juan de Fuca and back into the northern Pacific Ocean, skirting most of the group of rugged, densely forested islands that in 1867 would be named the Alexander Archipelago, in honor of Tsar Alexander II. As the *Boyatyr* neared Sitka, those on board sighted Mount Edgecumbe, half-covered with snow and girdled by clouds. Fifteen miles west of Sitka, on Kruzof Island, Mount Edgecumbe had been given its name by British Captain James Cook in 1778. The more than 3,200-foot-tall extinct volcano that towered over the approach to the harbor had earlier been named Mount St. Lazaria by Russian naval explorer Alexi Ilich Chirikov in 1741. As the *Bogatyr* entered Sitka Sound on May 14, making its way through the small islands into Sitka Harbor, Admiral Popov probably marveled again at the system of cables that made for safe anchorage, even in the worst of weather. The harbor also boasted Russian America's only lighthouse, a light in the cupola of the pitched roof house of the chief manager, known as Baranov's Castle, which, with six polished reflectors behind it, could be seen at night for twenty miles. In the harbor when the *Bogatyr* arrived was the Russian-American Company's screw-driven 1,200-ton steamship *Alexander II*.

Upon arrival the prince and his family debarked. Governor Furuhelm and his wife, Anna Elisabeth, welcomed them. Maksutov presented his new bride and was reunited with his very young son, Aleksandr, who had been cared for by the Furuhelms while the prince was in Russia. One of their first visits would undoubtedly have been to the grave of the prince's first wife, Adelaide, the mother of his daughters. All three of the prince's children had been born in Sitka during the prince's time as the assistant chief manager (1859–1863). The princess died of what was then called a "galloping consumption" on December 19, 1862, three months after the birth of their third child, Alexandr. She was buried in a small Lutheran cemetery at Sitka alongside Edvard Etolin, the infant son of Gov. Adolf Etolin and his wife, Margareta, and the brother of Lieutenant Etolin of the *Bogatyr*. Her burial spot was marked by a marble grave marker that had been shipped from Russia. Admiral Popov more than likely accompanied the prince as he walked up the small hill to this solemn site in the Lutheran cemetery overlooking Sitka. It is also possible that Lieutenant Etolin went to visit the grave of his infant brother, which was marked by a cast iron cross.

New Archangel / Sitka was a town of some twenty-five hundred people by this time, of whom only about four hundred were Russians. Yet these were over half of all the Russians in Russian America. The town boasted a shipyard as well as Russian-American Company warehouses and workshops, most painted yellow, with their sheet-iron roofs painted red. It also contained two sawmills, a flouring mill, a brickyard, a foundry, machine shops, bakeries, and a tannery. Private residences were situated on side streets. These side streets, as with all the streets in the town, had board sidewalks.

Popov had come again to this outpost of Russian "civility" in North America. It had leisurely public gardens and teahouses. The upper story of the castle had been converted into a theater. The plays were in French as well as Russian. There were musical evenings, dances, and when important visitors, such as Admiral Popov, came and on important holidays there were balls given by the chief manager and his lady at their residence. Popov had earlier criticized these social customs. After a visit in 1862 he wrote to Admiral-General and Grand Duke Konstatin about the Russian-American Company's extravagant squandering of resources on such pastimes. He was especially critical of a lavish ball given during his visit, which was attended by more than forty ladies.[3]

There was an excellent public library, which contained several thousand volumes in most European languages. It contained a college, as well as two scientific institutes, one of natural history and the other of ethnography. There was also a forty-bed hospital and associated outpatient clinic and pharmacy, serving annually about two thousand persons.

New Archangel was also the site of the little Orthodox Cathedral of Saint Michael (the Archangel), seat of Bishop Innocent's (Veniaminov's) successor, Bishop Peter (Lysakov). Dedicated on November 20, 1848, it replaced the old church built during the Baranov era. The cross-shaped cathedral contained a chime of bells, a gift from the Church at Moscow, that was worthy of any shrine. The belfry clock was said to be the work of the hands of Veniaminov. Bishop Peter, the former rector of the Sitka Seminary, had been appointed Auxiliary Bishop for Sitka in 1859 when Bishop Innocent had transferred his see to Siberia.[4] There were two other churches at the time. One was a Lutheran church, built in 1843 during the governorship of Arvid Adolf Etolin, a Finnish Lutheran and the father of one the officers in

Popov's squadron, Lt. Alexander Etolin, aboard the *Bogatyr*. This Lutheran church contained the first pipe organ on the west coast of North America, manufactured in 1844 in Estonia and shipped to Sitka in 1846. The other church was on the line of the stockade that separated the Russian settlement from the Tlingit settlement. It had two doors, one inside the fortification, the other outside and used as an entrance by the natives. Although officially named the Church of the Holy Resurrection, the Russians knew it as the Koloshian or Tlinget Church. It had earlier been known as the Church of the Holy Life-Creating Trinity. However, even with all these amenities, Sitka had no streetlights, so after dark the residents went about with lanterns.

The town was dominated by the largest building in the city, which occupied the top of the hill, a rocky promontory fifty-two feet above the sea, overlooking the harbor. It was the rambling two-story yellow house of the chief manager, built in 1837. Atop its pitched roof, covered with sheet iron, sat the only lighthouse in Russian-America. Its light was said to be visible for twenty miles. Intended not only as a residence, but also as a refuge, it was commonly called "Baranov's Castle," after the earlier structure occupied by the famed founder of the settlement, Aleksandr Andreevich Baranov, even though its construction was initiated some eighteen years after Baranov's departure from Sitka. A thick wooden wall covered with sheet iron surrounded the house. Out of the sides were mounted forty cannons, varying from twelve- to twenty-four-pounders, ready for use in case of Indian attack or an attack from a ship in the harbor. On the line of the stockade were three blockhouses. This "castle" served in many ways as the center of social life in Sitka. A large room had movable partitions so it could be turned into a ballroom. Admiral Popov and his officers would have been received and entertained there, and would have noticed the furniture of sufficient quality to impress any visitor.

Prince Maksutov, who had arrived aboard the *Bogatyr*, would be the final governor of Russian America. Less than a year later, in April 1865, Captain Scammon and the *Shubrick* would visit Sitka and pay a call on the Prince as a part of the navy expedition supporting the Russian and American Telegraph Company. In the summer of 1867 the United States Senate would vote to purchase the territory from Russia. Prince Maksutov would order the Russian flag hauled down in October 18, 1867, transferring ownership to the United States and ending a more than 120-year Russian presence in North America.

Upon arrival at Sitka, Admiral Popov learned that the Russian-American Company's steamship *Alexander II* was about to sail to the Okhotsk Sea. He secured permission and funding from the prince to send Lieutenant Abzheltovsky and Midshipman Makarov aboard the *Alexander II*, so that they could report to their new assignments at Petrovsky on the Amur River.

The day before the outgoing governor, Finnish-born Ivan Furuhelm and his wife Anna were to depart, Prince Maksutov gave them an elaborate farewell ball.

Before departing on May 18, the *Bogatyr* took aboard the outgoing governor, for the return to trip to San Francisco.

On this return trip the *Bogatyr* again visited Vancouver to secure provisions and supplies at lower costs than available in San Francisco. They would stay at Vancouver from May 27 to June 4. This visit pleased their distinguished passenger, former governor Furuhelm, who welcomed the opportunity to get to know his British neighbors. Departing on June 4 the *Bogatyr* returned to San Francisco on June 8.

While the *Bogatyr* was in Sitka delivering the new governor and his family, the *Shubrick* was ordered to northern waters. *Joseph Lane,* which had arrived on April 28 from Puget Sound, commenced acting as the guard ship for San Francisco harbor. Commanded by Lt. James M. Selden, the 102-foot topsail schooner, built in 1849 in Portsmouth, Virginia, had no steam power. However, the *Joseph Lane* was considered one of the fastest and most graceful schooners of the clipper ship days. Originally named *Campbell*, in 1855 her name was changed to *Joseph Lane*. For armament she carried one eighteen-pounder and two thirty-two-pounders.[5]

It was not just Americans in San Francisco that feared an attack by a rebel cruiser. On May 12 the master of a Dutch merchant ship, anchored in San Francisco Bay, advised the commanding officer of the USS *Saranac*, which was acting as the guard ship at the time, that a suspicious vessel was cruising off the port; that a pilot boat was seen to communicate, then both vessels headed seaward and disappeared. The Dutch master presumed that the suspicious vessel was a rebel privateer and had captured the pilot boat. The *Saranac* got underway and headed out to sea to search for the suspicious vessel. Unable to locate the vessel and discovering that the pilot boat had safely returned to her former anchorage, the *Saranac* returned to port.[6]

About six o'clock on the evening of May 20 another very heavy earthquake struck San Francisco. A local newspaper reported it as "one of the heaviest, if not absolutely the heaviest, earthquake ever felt in San Francisco."[7] It lasted between ten and twenty seconds. No buildings cracked, and there was no significant damage. Locals took it in stride, but strangers, including probably a number of the Russian sailors, were somewhat scared. A few days later a local newspaper reported another danger that the Russian sailors had to face while in San Francisco.

> On Saturday last, a Russian sailor with an unpronounceable name, but ending with the orthodoxy "sky", while enjoying a short leave of absence from his ship wandered into a classic locality in the vicinity of Pacific and Dupont streets, and entering a saloon, came out. . . . With the next thing to a broken head. Witnesses testified that the barkeep asked the sailor to pay for three drinks, and when the cash was not immediately forthcoming. The bartender took a cane and "very rudely whacked

him over the head with it." The cane was produced in court and was an ugly weapon. . . .
After a short hearing the matter was continued by the Judge for further consideration.[8]

On May 30 San Franciscans rejoiced when the
first gun from the batteries at Angel Island, one of the
new ten-inch Columbiads received from the East, was
fired by a detachment of the Third U.S. Artillery. The
ship *Nesuton* delivered a total of four fifteen-inch and
two ten-inch guns for harbor defenses. The remainder
of the guns were mounted within a few days.[9] The following month San Franciscans would welcome the news
that the feared Confederate commerce raider *Alabama*,
which had roamed the seas and destroyed or captured sixty-
four American merchant ships, was sunk by the USS
Kearsarge off of Cherbourg, France on June 19, 1864.

A reminder of the city's continuing fear occurred
on Friday evening, June 18, when army sentinels at
Alcatraz fired upon a boat that was headed for Angel
Island. The boat had started from the City Front under
sail, but the wind slackened just before it reached the pre-
scribed distance of five hundred yards from the island.
The sail was hauled down, and the oars shipped, when
it made almost directly towards the landing, instead of
running outside the line of five hundred yards from the
island.[10] It later was discovered to be an excursion boat.

Dr. C. M. Hitchcock, a lady, and the four soldiers
who occupied the boat were going up to Angel Island
when the sentinel on Alcatraz hailed them from his post.

An immediate reply was reportedly given, but the sentinel, not hearing it, hailed again and immediately afterward fired his musket, hitting one of the oarsmen (named Nugent) in his left arm. The sentinel again hailed after the firing and asked the occupants where they were going, to which Dr. Hitchcock replied, "To take ashore the man you've shot!" The officer at Alcatraz came down to the landing as the wounded man was brought ashore. The officer later stated that he had heard the hail of the boat's party, even though farther away from it than the sentinel. He also noted that the moon was shining clearly and brightly.

Captain Winder, the commanding officer of Alcatraz, promptly investigated and found that the sentinel had acted in accordance with instructions from the War Department. Those instructions had been made known to the public by advertisements in the local papers of San Francisco some months before. Captain Winder stated that had even he, the commandant of Alcatraz, been aboard the boat, he could not have been permitted to approach within five hundred yards of the island without giving the countersign and then lying to until the officer of the day had been notified of the fact, and ordered the sentinel to allow the landing. Captain Winder stated that had the excursion boat, on being hailed, laid back on their oars until the circumstances had been reported to the officer of the day, they would have been in no difficulty and could have then gone on their way unmolested. As it was, two other sentinels had already brought their muskets to bear on the boat, and would probably have fired in another instant, had not the officer of the day arrived to give orders to the contrary.

On Tuesday morning, June 21, the USS *Saranac* sent a small boat to the Russian flagship, *Bogatyr*, which had recently returned to the harbor. A little over an hour later the *Saranac* fired a thirteen-gun salute to Admiral Popov, which was returned by the *Bogatyr*. Shortly after that the *Bogatyr* fired a twenty-one-gun national salute to the harbor, which the *Saranac* returned, gun for gun, rather than Fort Alcatraz.

A few days later, on Friday, June 24, the city was struck by a severe storm. The morning was warm and pleasant, but shortly after noon the sea breeze set in through the Golden Gate and by half-past three had increased to a regular gale, which prevailed with only slight abatement until nearly sunset. About four o'clock, the clipper ship *Game Cock*, which was lying in the stream off the Vallejo Street wharf, hoisted the signal of distress, and it was observed that she was dragging her anchors and drifting rapidly toward Yerba Buena Island. The USS. *Saranac* immediately dispatched one of its small cutters to assist the *Game Cock*.

The captain of the *Game Cock*, who was on shore at the moment, seeing the peril of his vessel, started in company with others on board the plunger sloop *John C. Heenan* to go on board. When the *Heenan* had sailed about halfway down the slip between Pacific and Broadway wharves, with all sail set, she was struck by a sudden squall, thrown on her beam ends, and sunk instantly in some twenty feet of water. The captain and his friends swam for Broadway wharf. When they reached the piles, they were pulled up on the wharf by the bystanders— damp, but otherwise in a good state of preservation. A second start was made on the *Pride of the Bay*, and in eight minutes Captain Shelly, the pilot, was on board the vessel. Meantime the *Game Cock* was drifting nearer and nearer the rocky point of Yerba Buena, and without intervention would have inevitably gone to pieces.

Admiral Popov, recently returned from Sitka and seeing the *Game Cock's* situation, had the launches of the *Bogatyr* immediately lowered and manned, but rightly judged that she would need more assistance than the boats' crews could give her and signaled to the war steamer *Abrek* to go at once to her aid. At 5:45 p.m. the *Abrek*, steam up and anchors hoisted in a few minutes, arrived at the *Game Cock* at the same time as the merchant steamer *Goliah*. The two vessels soon had the *Game Cock* towed out to the southward by the island into a position where her anchors would hold her in safety. The commanders of the *Narragansett* and the *Saranac*, although short handed, had also each sent a boat's crew to the aid of the *Game Cock*. About sunset, the *Goliah* went over to tow her back to her anchorage in the stream.

The following day the *Alta California*'s report on the incident concluded with these words:

> The promptness with which Admiral Popoff [*sic*] and his officers acted in the matter of relieving the vessel from her perilous posi-

tion was the subject of very general and flattering comments among the shippers, merchants, and seafaring men of our city last evening, and it certainly will not abate the feeling of friendliness and good will towards our Russian visitors already entertained by all classes of our people.[11]

Admiral Popov would be present for the city's Fourth of July celebration. On that national holiday all U.S. ships were full dressed, with all their flag and pennants flying. U.S. Navy and Revenue Cutter Service vessels also fired a twenty-one-gun salute beginning at noon, as specified in their regulations. Other ships frequently decorated themselves as well. Virtually every ship in harbor, of all sizes and descriptions and nationalities, were profusely decorated for the day. The Russian *Bogatyr* displayed more than one hundred fifty flags, and was the best decorated ship in the harbor. A local paper declared that *Bogatyr* was, "justly entitled to the palm over all competitors."[12]

The day began with the city being awaked by a national salute fired by the artillery of the California Guard. The whole city was swathed in a waving drapery of flags. Scarcely a house or business could be found without a flag or bunting.

The chief feature of the day was a grand parade. By eleven o'clock the parade was formed and began to move. The huge parade began with a military division, so large that it took thirteen minutes to pass a given point. Included in the second division of the immense parade were forty carriages, containing foreign consuls, Admiral Popov, the USN officers then in port, officers of the *Narragansett*, officers of the US Army and Navy, Customhouse officers, members of the board of supervisors, and other city and county officials. Next in line were the public schools with their bands and banners. Then came the benevolent societies and after these followed numerous carriages containing citizens, and behind them citizens on foot ended the long procession. It passed Portsmouth Square, then went downhill, through Washington Street, finally going down Montgomery Street and disbanding in the vicinity of the Metropolitan Theatre, where the concluding ceremonies took place.

The day ended with a huge fireworks display set up at the corner of Fifth and Harrison Streets. Between thirteen and fifteen thousand persons gathered to see what Mark Twain, writing for the San Francisco *Daily Morning Call*, described as "by far the most magnificent spectacle of the kind ever witnessed on the Pacific coast." He went on to conclude by saying, "A number of balls and parties and a terrific cannonade of fire crackers, kept up all night long, finished the festivities of this memorable Fourth of July in San Francisco."[13]

Shortly afterward the *Abrek,* with Admiral Popov and his staff aboard, together with the *Kalevala*, sailed for a cruise in the Central Pacific. Their first port was to be Honolulu.[14]

The summer of 1864 would see other military and naval changes. On the first of July Maj. Gen. Irvin McDowell, the Union general who earlier in the war had been blamed in part for the disaster at the Second Battle of Bull Run, arrived in San Francisco to take command of the Department of the Pacific.

On the morning of July 13 General McDowell, accompanied by his staff and many military officers, officials, and civilians, including Governor Low, the collector of the port, and several members of the press, boarded the *Goliah* for a tour of the harbor's defenses. The *Goliah* departed from the Broadway wharf and steamed down the bay toward Fort Point. Upon arrival at the fort the vessel was received with an appropriate gun salute to General McDowell. From the barbette, practice shells were fired, intended to reach the opposite shore at Lime Point. However, defective fuses caused the shells to explode almost immediately upon leaving the guns. The *Goliah*, with its distinguished guests, then steamed close along the shore of Lime Point to examine the location of a hoped for future fortification. From there the vessel steamed to Angel Island to view the beginning preparations for a future battery to guard the bay. The *Goliah* next took its distinguished passengers to Fort Alcatraz for an inspection of that fortress and then steamed to Yerba Buena Island, another position that had not yet been fortified. The *Goliah* then passed up the bay to the mouth of Mission Creek, past the *Aquilla*, returned to the Broadway wharf, and was greeted by a band.[15]

Toward the end of July General McDowell visited the USS *Saranac,* the vessel then acting as the official guard ship of the harbor. On July 27, Captain Charles Poor, of the *Saranac*, the senior U.S. naval officer present in the harbor, paid a visit to the *Bogatyr,* which had gotten underway and proceeded to Saucelito. Captain Poor was received aboard the *Bogatyr* with the appropriate eleven-gun salute, which was returned by the *Saranac*.

The following day Admiral Ivan Andreevich Endsgurov and his staff officers, Malofayov and Oussov, arrived aboard the Pacific Mail Steamship Company's steamer *Uncle Sam* to make preparations to take command of the Russian squadron from Admiral Popov. They took apartments at the Occidental Hotel for their temporary lodging. On August 4 the *Abrek* and *Kalevala* arrived from Honolulu. The *Abrek*, aboard which Admiral Popov had sailed to Honolulu, arrived in the morning. Later in the day, about four o'clock in the afternoon, Admiral Popov arrived aboard *Kalevala* and received the usual salutes from the ships in the harbor. Beyond the salutes there was no celebration since the day was being observed throughout the United States as a day of fasting, humiliation, and prayer, as directed by President Lincoln. Public offices, courts, schools, banks, and most places of business were closed and church-going San Franciscans assembled at their places of worship.

As the day for the Russians' departure grew near, the *Alta California* newspaper expressed the feelings of many San Franciscans.

The reception which was given to the Admiral and the officers of his fleet, on their arrival in our port, was one of the most cordial character, and during the time they were among us they have, by their uniform courtesy and gentlemanly demeanor, and their repeated acts of generosity and voluntary efforts to save the property of our people from destruction by fire and storm, increased the feeling of friendliness and respect entertained by our people for themselves and the people to which they belong, and the Government which they represent. Our people will witness with regret, and will look forward with pleasing anticipations of their return to our shores in the—we trust, not distant—future.[16]

On the day before the Russians departed, the *Alta California* wrote of the soon to depart Russian officers and men, saying,

Whilst we regret the departure, not alone of Admiral Popoff [*sic*], but his successor and fleet, we take occasion to say that few, if any, foreign nations have been so ably represented in our midst. The officers and men have won the esteem of all by their truly admiral conduct. The officers, as gentlemen of refinement and education, will leave behind them

hosts of friends, and the men, from their or-
derly conduct, have won universal respect.
Success to them.[17]

That same day Christian Andres' Band at the Russ
House serenaded Admiral Popov at a concert in his
honor. The Russ House, one of San Francisco's best
hotels, had opened just two years earlier, in 1862. On
August 13, Russia's Pacific Squadron departed San
Francisco, under their new commander, Admiral
Endsgurov. They sailed to the Sandwich Islands and
from there to Japan, and then home to their native land.
About the same time that the Russian ships left, Admiral Popov took passage on the steamer *Golden City* for
Panama. The *Golden City*, with an unusually small number of passengers, departed from the Folsom Street wharf
at about ten o'clock. As Admiral Popov departed, the crews
of the civilian steamers also loudly cheered him, and the
yards and rigging of the vessels were manned in honor
of the new commander of the fleet, Admiral Endsgurov.
The Russian squadron acted as an escort for Admiral
Popov aboard the *Golden City*. As the Russian fleet
passed Alcatraz and Fort Point, they fired national salutes and flew the American colors from their foremasts.
The batteries of Alcatraz also saluted Admiral Popov
as the *Golden City* passed by. When beyond the Golden
Gate, the Russian squadron fired an admiral's salute as
a "good-bye" to their former commander.

By the fall of 1864, most of the fear of San
Franciscans had abated. The Confederate commerce

raider *Alabama* had been sunk by the USS *Kearsarge* off Cherbourg, France on June 12 and the *Florida* was captured by the USS *Wachusett* off Brazil in October. Only the commerce raider *Shenandoah* remained. Atlanta would fall to the army of General William Tecumseh Sherman on September 1. The outcome of the Civil War was no longer in doubt. No one seriously feared British or French intervention this late in the war. While regretting the departure of the Russian Pacific Squadron, the U.S. Navy was now taking more responsibility for the defense of the harbor.

In mid-November the USS *Wateree*, a 205-foot iron side-wheel gunboat reached San Francisco to serve in the Pacific Squadron and relieve the *Saranac* as the guard ship for the harbor. The double-ended gunboat *Wateree* was one of the strangest ships that San Franciscans had ever seen. Built especially for service on the sounds and rivers of the southern states, the *Wateree* had no pretensions to seaworthiness or to efficiency as a cruiser. The only qualities this river gunboat possessed were heavy guns. However, upon her arrival in San Francisco, the *Wateree* entered the Mare Island Naval Shipyard for repairs of damage suffered during her difficult voyage and for a hull scraping. She would not leave the shipyard until late February 1865, and then to patrol the coast of Central America.

During the winter of 1864–65 the *Shenandoah* cruised the whaling grounds in the Pacific and off Alaska, destroying much of the U. S. whaling fleet. In May the captain of the *Shenandoah*, James Waddell, learned of Richmond's fall from a newspaper taken from a captured whaler. The article also said that Confederate President Jefferson Davis had insisted that the war would go on, so the *Shenandoah* continued her mission of destruction. That summer the *Shenandoah* headed south towards California, toying with a plan to attack the shipping at San Francisco or even launch a daring raid on San Francisco itself. Waddell's plan was to run past Fort Point at night, ram and disable the navy's guard ship, and turn his guns on San Francisco. Artillerymen at Fort Point and Alcatraz were ready, but they waited in vain for the *Shenandoah*. In early August the captain of the *Shenandoah* learned from newspapers on a British ship thirteen days out of San Francisco that Lee and Johnston had surrendered, all the armies in the field gone, Jefferson Davis was imprisoned in irons, and the navies of the world were searching the seas for the *Shenandoah*—a ship without a country. The *Shenandoah* turned away from San Francisco and made its way back to Liverpool under British colors where it surrendered to British authorities in November 1865.

7

EPILOGUE

The goodwill engendered by the visit from Russia's Pacific Squadron lasted for many years. After the end of the Civil War, Admiral Popov and many of his officers had the opportunity to express their appreciation for San Francisco's hospitality. Just one year after the assassination of President Lincoln, an attempt was made on the life of the Russian tsar, Alexander II. The American government, learning of this attempt, sent a delegation headed by the assistant secretary of the navy, Gustavus Vasa Fox, to St. Petersburg. Fox and his party were transported to Kronstadt by a special naval detachment consisting of the monitor *Miantonomah* and the steamer *Augusta*.

At the Russian Merchant's Society for Mutual Assistance dinner on August 7, Fox responded to a toast offered by the Russians by saying, "We are the guests of a society whose designation is 'mutual assistance.' May these words be prophetic of the future moral relations of Russia and America! The significant sympathies which Russia offered to the United States during our struggle for the Union will always be remembered and reciprocated." Admiral Popov was present at the Peterhof Palace in St. Petersburg on August 8, 1866, when Fox formally presented the resolution of Congress that expressed the thankfulness of the American people for Russia's support during the Civil War and for Tsar Alexander II's providential escape from assassination. After Fox had delivered the resolution to the tsar, the emperor responded in Russian. Prince Gortchakov, minister of foreign affairs, translated his words into English as follows:

> His Majesty said that he rejoices at the friendly relations existing between Russia and the United States, and he is pleased to see that those relations are so well appreciated in America. He is convinced that the national fraternity will be perpetual, and he, for his part, will contribute efforts to sustain it, and to strengthen the bonds. He is deeply sensible of the proofs of the personal sympathy and affection of the American people, conveyed in the Resolution of Congress, and he is grateful for them. He desires to thank those who have come so great a distance to bear these proofs to him, and he assures them of a warm welcome to the soil of Russia.

His Majesty adds that the cordial reception given to his squadron in the United
States will never be effaced from his
memory.[1]

Later, the members of the American naval delegation were the guests of honor at a dinner given by
the Kronstadt Naval Club. The invitations stated that
the Russian officers "desired to express the sentiments
of friendship they bear toward the citizens of the United
States, as well as to show their appreciation of the
warmth and heartiness of the reception accorded to the
Russian fleets in the cities of New York, Washington,
Boston and San Francisco."[2]

At another dinner given by Prince Valdimir
Andreevich Dolgorukov, the governor general of Moscow, the prince said in his welcoming address to the
delegation, "The brilliant reception given by the United
States to the Russian squadron in 1863 and 1864 has
left in Russian hearts an ineffaceable remembrance of
gratitude, and has drawn together still more closely, if
possible, the ties of love and of sympathy which united
the two nations."[3]

At the merchant's dinner at the Great Fair in
Nizhni Novgorod, on the banks of the Volga River, Mr.
Schipov, the president of the fair, declared, "I thank our
dear American visitors for the kind reception their country gave our Russian naval officers. When Russia was
experiencing a dark hour, America showed her sympathy
in unmistakable signs, and Kronstadt, St. Petersburg and

Moscow have been trying to return similar evidences of friendship."[4]

A farewell breakfast for Mr. Fox's mission was given aboard Admiral Krabbe's yacht, *Rurik*, on Saturday, September 15. Among the Russian guests was Rear Admiral Popov. The *Rurik* was decorated with the flags of both nations and a band played the national airs. As soon as the champagne was served, Vice Admiral Krabbe, who as chief of the tsar's Imperial Navy had ordered Rear Admiral Popov to take his fleet to San Francisco, rose and began his remarks by stating, "You remember, gentlemen, with what attention and enthusiasm we followed the news of the reception in America of Admirals Lesovskii and Popov. At last Heaven has allowed us to thank our guests personally for their hospitality."[5]

Just a few months after Fox's delegation returned to the United States, the long-pending negotiations for the sale of Alaska were concluded. The goodwill between Russia and the United States undoubtedly influenced Russia to sell Alaska to the United States, and also probably influenced Congress to agree to the purchase. Many had initially considered Alaska to be a frozen, barren wasteland. Some, at the time, believed the money was really a payment for the expenses the Russians had incurred during the time their ships were in U.S. harbors. Russia transferred nearly six hundred thousand square miles of her territory to the United States for a trifling sum of money—$7.2 million in gold. The United States took formal possession of Alaska on October 18, 1867, at Sitka, when the double-eagle emblem of Russia was lowered and replaced by the Stars and Stripes.

A few years later, in 1871, Grand Duke Alexis Alexandrovich, the twenty-two-year-old fourth son of Tsar Alexander II, visited the United States at the invitation of President Ulysesses Grant. The Grand Duke visited the President at the White House and spent three months visiting thirty-four towns, starting in New York and finishing his good will visit in New Orleans. He visited Chicago shortly after its Great Fire and gave $5,000 in gold (equivalent to $250,000 today) to help the homeless people of that city. Grand Duke Alexis was met everywhere with genuine enthusiasm as a representative of Russia—"our steadfast and unswerving friend." During a parade on Broadway in New York he was welcomed as a "Representative of this Nation's dearly cherished ally." The official part of his visit was followed by hunting buffalo in Nebraska together with Lt. Gen. Philip Sheridan and Lt. Col. George Custer, accompanied by the United States Cavalry and one thousand Souix Indians with their chief, Spotted Tail. The Grand Duke's chief hunting guide was the legendary William "Buffalo Bill" Cody.[6]

Andrei Aleksandrovich Popov

Rear Admiral Popov returned to Russia to be present on August 8, 1866, at Peterhof Palace when an American delegation formally presented the resolution of Congress that expressed the thankfulness of the American people for Russia's support during the Civil

War and for Tsar Alexander II's providential escape
from assassination. He went on to design many warships, including the circular "Popovkas," the *Novgorod*
and *Rear-Admiral Popov*, and the *Tchesma* and *Sinope*
classes. In 1872, under his direction, Russia produced
the world's largest and most powerful turret battleship,
Pyotr Veliky (Peter the Great), with a displacement of
10,105 tons; in 1873, they produced the world's first
armored cruiser, the 5,300-ton frigate *General-Admiral*. Promoted to vice admiral in 1872 and full admiral
in 1891, Popov died in March 1898. Popof Glacier, a
half-mile southeast of Mt. Basargin and nineteen miles
northeast of Wrangell, was named for him in 1863 by a
surveying party from the *Rynda* on the Stikine River.

Joseph Lanman

Commodore Joseph Lanman, commander of Ad-
miral Bell's flagship, the *Lancaster*, departed San Francisco the same month as Admiral Popov. Lanman headed
east to command the *Minnesota* in the North Atlantic
Blocking Squadron. Lanman returned to the *Lancaster*
in his final tour of duty as commander of the South Atlantic Squadron, from June 1869 to May 1872, when
he retired. He died at his home in Norwich, Connecti-
cut, on March 18, 1874.

Charles H. Bell

Rear Admiral Bell relinquished command of the
U.S. Navy's Pacific Squadron to Rear Adm. George F.
Pearson in October 1864 and returned to his home to

await orders. In July 1865 Bell was appointed commander of the East India Squadron. He later commanded the New York Navy Yard. Bell retired in 1869 and died on February 19, 1875, in New Brunswick, New Jersey, where he was buried.

Thomas O. Selfridge, Sr.

That same October, Commodore Selfridge relinquished command of the Mare Island Navy Yard and awaited orders until January 1866, when he took command of the Philadelphia Navy Yard. Then a rear admiral, Selfridge returned to Mare Island in September of 1872 for his final tour of duty in the Navy, and retired in June 1873. He died in his native Massachusetts on October 15, 1902, at the age of ninety-three. The British admiralty ordered their ships and stations to fly their flags at half-mast in his memory. Selfridge was the oldest admiral in the world when he died.

During the Civil War, Commodore Selfridge's son, Thomas O. Selfridge, Jr., commanded the *Monitor* and the experimental submarine *Alligator*, and he had the unwanted distinction of being the only Union naval officer during the war to have three ships sunk under him. The *Cumberland* went down while engaging the Confederate ironclad *Virginia* during the March 8, 1862, battle in Hampton Roads; the monitor *Cairo* sank in the Yazoo River after a torpedo exploded under her hull; and the gunboat *Conestoga* was lost in the Mississippi River after a collision.

Charles M. Scammon

The same month the Russian squadron departed San Francisco, Charles M. Scammon, commanding officer of the *Shubrick*, was promoted to the rank of captain in the Revenue Cutter Service. That October, Captain Scammon and the *Shubrick* returned to San Francisco to resume boarding ships; rescuing those in trouble; and serving, along with the USS *Saranac*, as the guardian of the port. Scammon remained in command of the *Shubrick* until April 1865. He then went on to a long and distinguished career commanding a number of other revenue cutters. Captain Scammon also gained fame in the scientific community with the publication of his *Marine Mammals of the Northwestern Coast of North America*. First published in 1874, it became one of the major primary sources for information about whales in the nineteenth century. It remains a premier source for the historical and scientific development of cetology and mammalogy, and for historians of whaling and sealing. After retiring from the Revenue Cutter Service in 1895, Scammon died in 1911 at his home in Oakland, California, and is buried beside his wife in the Evergreen Cemetery there. Scammon Lagoon, on the west coast of Baja California Sur, is one of the prime breeding grounds of the gray whale in Baja California, and is named for him.

Alexander Adolphovich Etolin

Lieutenant Alexander Adophovich Etolin returned on vacation to the United States in February of 1872 to

marry Katherine Selfridge, the daughter of Commodore
Selfridge and Etolin's former English teacher at Mare
Island. The couple was married in Washington, DC,
and they made their home near St. Petersburg. Their
son, Alexander, was born on January 3, 1873. Etolin
died in August 1901, and his wife died in March 1925
in Helsinki.

Stepan O. Makarov

Stepan O. Makarov, the young midshipman who
also studied English with Commodore Selfridge's
daughter, went on to have a distinguished career in the
Russian navy. As a rear admiral and commander of the
Russian Pacific Navy in the Russo-Japanese War,
Makarov perished when his flagship, the *Petropavlovsk,*
hit a mine and sank. The Russian State Maritime University in St. Petersburg is named in his honor.

Dmitrii Petrovich Maksutov

Prince Maksutov and his young wife were present
at the transfer of Alaska to U.S. control. The Princess
Maksutova fainted when the Russian flag caught on its
pole, refusing to be lowered. She, along with five children (three by the prince's first wife, and two of whom
she had borne while in Sitka) and their nurse, departed
in January 1868 for Panama, New York, and ultimately
Russia. While en route to Russia, the older of her own
sons, Vladimir, died. She had two more children in St.
Petersburg—Mariia, born in 1876, and Olga, born in 1877.
A year passed before Prince Maksutov could return home.

The week following the princess's departure, he had to travel to San Francisco on legal business connected with the sale of company property. He did not depart San Francisco until March 31. He remained in Sitka until January 6, 1869, when he sailed for San Francisco on the bark *Menshikov*. By April 30 of that year he was back on the family estate at Tula. In June 1881 his wife, then only thirty-six years old, died. Maksutov himself died on March 21, 1889, and is buried in St. Petersburg.

The Six Russian Sailors

The six Russian sailors who lost their lives fighting the October 1863 fire in San Francisco were buried with full military honors in the Mare Island Cemetery and were left behind when Admiral Popov and his Russian squadron sailed home in August 1864. For the next 141 years, their graves lay almost unnoticed in the cemetery filled with the graves of American navy service members. However, in January 1994, when the Russian training ship *Admiral Nevelskoi* arrived in San Francisco as part of an around-the-world voyage from the Vladivostok Maritime Academy, they were remembered. Captain Leonid Lysenko knew of the 1863 visit and tracked down the graves' location. On Tuesday, January 25, while a steady rain fell, Lysenko, two Russian Orthodox priests, members of the San Francisco Russian consulate, and several residents of the Russian-American community gathered at their graves. The Rev. Victor Sokolov, a Russian émigré and rector of Trinity Orthodox Cathedral in San Francisco, presided at a ceremony at the cemetery to pray for the souls of those six Russian sailors. "For so long their names were forgotten, but their deeds were not. They died protecting the citizens of San Francisco and according to the Gospel, putting their lives on the line for their neighbors." Sokolov was assisted by the Rev. Alexander Karpenko of St. Nicholas Russian (Patriarchal) Orthodox Church of San Francisco. Deputy Russian Consul Vladimir Golubkov pointed to the squadron's historical visit as one of "all the good things [that have happened] between the two of us."[7]

Mare Island Cemetery, final resting place of six Russian sailors who lost their lives fighting the October 1863 fire in San Francisco

NOTES

Chapter 1: Russian-American Relations at the Time of the Civil War

1. Dean B. Mahin, *One War at a Time* (Washington, DC: Brassey's, 1999), 58–82.

2. Nikolai N. Bolkhovitinov, *The Beginnings of Russian-American Relations, 1775–1815* (Cambridge, MA: Harvard University Press, 1975), 3–29.

3. Ibid., 65–74.

4. Frank Golder, "Russian-American Relations During the Crimean War," *American Historical Review* 31, no. 3 (April 1926): 470–471.

5. Ibid., 474.

6. Horace Bell, *Reminiscences of a Ranger, or Early Times in Southern California* (Santa Barbara, CA: Wallace Hebberd, 1927), 425–426.

7. Gortchakov to Taylor, October 1862, in B. B. Sideman and L. Friedman, eds., *Europe Looks at the Civil War* (New York: Collier Books, 1962), 184.

8. Charles A. De Arnaud, *The Union, and Its Ally, Russia* (Washington, DC: Gibson, 1890), 21.

9. San Francisco *Evening Daily Bulletin*, February 7, 1864.

10. "Russia and the United States," *Sacramento Union*, October 29, 1863.

11. *Alta California,* February 28, 1863.

12. Arkhiv Morskogo Ministerstva, *Dielo Kantseliarii Morskogo Ministerstva*, no. 109, pt I, cited by Frank Golder in "The Russian Fleet and the Civil War," *American Historical Review*, 20 (1915): 804.

13. Ibid.

14. V. Fitzharding, "Russian Naval Visitors to Australia, 1862–1888," *Journal of the Royal Australian Historical Society* 52, part 2 (1966).

15. *Morskoi Sbornik*, October 1914, 35–40.

16. *Evening Daily Bulletin*, November 18, 1863.

Chapter 2: San Francisco's Fear

1. Rockwell D. Hunt and Nellie Van De Grift Sánchez, *A Short History of California* (New York: Thomas Y. Crowell Company, 1929), 420.

2. Oscar Lewis, *The War in the Far West: 1861–1865* (Garden City, NJ: Doubleday, 1961), 236.

3. Navy Department, *Official Records of the Union and Confederate Navies in the War of the Rebellion,* series 1, vol. 1, part 2 (Washington, DC: 1894–1922), 108–109.

4. Bell to Welles, April 4, 1862, in Letters received from Pacific Squadron. National Archives and Records Administration, Washington, DC.

5. Selfridge to Welles, February 10, 1863. National Archives and Records Administration, Pacific Region, San Bruno, CA.

6. Report of Adj. General, California [William C. Kibbe], December 3, 1863. National Archives and Records Administration, Pacific Region, San Bruno, CA.

7. Commandant, Mare Island Naval Shipyard, to Secretary of the Navy, Letters Sent. National Archives and Records Administration, Pacific Region, San Bruno, CA.

8. Letter of February 20, 1863, *Records of War of Rebellion.*

9. Letter of April 25, 1863, *Records of War of Rebellion.*

10. Letter of April 27, 1863, *Records of War of Rebellion.*

11. Letter from Welles to J. B. Montgomery, April 27, 1861, *Records of War of Rebellion*, 15.

12. Arnold S. Lott, *A Long Line of Ships: Mare Island's Century of Naval Activity in California* (Annapolis, MD: Naval Institute Press, 1954), 78; "The Shubrick Incident," U.S. Coast Guard Academy *Alumni Association Bulletin* (March 1941).

13. Commandant, Mare Island Naval Shipyard, to Secretary of the Navy, Letters Sent, March 17, 1863. National Archives and Records Administration, Pacific Region, San Bruno, CA.

14. *Washington Standard* (Olympia), March 28, 1863.

15. *Alta California*, March 17, 1863.

16. *Alta California*, March 19, 1863.

17. Secretary of the Treasury, letter of July 1, 1863. National Archives and Records Administration, Washington, DC.

18. *Alta California*, August 1, 1863.

19. *Alta California*, March 1, 1864.

20. Ibid.

21. *San Francisco City Directory*, 1864.

22. *Alta California*, March 1, 1864.

23. Hymen R. Kaplan, "The U.S. Coast Guard and the Civil War," Naval Institute *Proceedings* 86, no. 8 (August 1960): 44.

24. *Alta California*, April 24, 1864.

25. David W. Shaw, *Sea Wolf of the Confederacy: The Daring Civil War Raids of Naval Lt. Charles W. Read* (New York: Free Press, 2004).

26. *Alta California*, July 31, 1863.

27. *San Francisco City Directory*, 1865.

28. Arkhiv Moskogo Ministerstva, *Dielo Kantseliarii Morskogo Ministerstva*, part. III, 102, 103, cited by Frank Golder in "The Russian Fleet and the Civil War," *American Historical Review* 20 (1915): 809.

29. *Morskoi Sbornik*, October 1914, 45.

Chapter 3: The Russians Arrive

1. *Alta California*, September 27, 1863.

2. Description of Revenue Cutter *Shubrick*. Dukes County Historical Society, Edgarton, MA.

3. *Shubrick* Log, January 1862.

4. Ibid., February 1862.

5. Ibid.

6. *Alta California*, September 28, 1863.

7. Ibid.

8. *Alta California*, October 18, 1863.

9. *Evening Daily Bulletin*, October 21, 1863.

10. Ibid., November 30, 1863.

11. Ibid., December 2, 1863.

12. *New York Times*, October 4, 1863.

13. Mairin Mitchell, *The Maritime History of Russia, 1848–1948* (London: Sidgwick and Jackson, 1949), 175.

14. Scammon Papers, Bancroft Library, University of California, 204: 3.

15. Frank A. Golder, "The Russian Fleet and the Civil War," *American Historical Review* 20 (1915): 808.

16. Popov Report of October 11, 1863, in Russian State Historic Archive, fond 410, inventory 2, file 2603, 522–527.

17. *Alta California*, October 16, 1863.

18. Mare Island Naval Shipyard Log.

19. *Alta California*, November 18, 1863.

Chapter 4: Mare Island

1. Arnold S. Lott, *A Long Line of Ships: Mare Island's Century of Naval Activity in California* (Annapolis, MD: Naval Institute Press, 1954), 82.

2. Ibid.

3. Mare Island Naval Shipyard Log.

4. *Alta California*, October 25, 1863.

5. Mare Island Naval Shipyard, Letters Sent, October 26, 1863.

6. Popov report of October 11, 1863, in Russian archives, St. Petersburg.

7. *Evening Daily Bulletin*, October 29, 1863.

8. *Alta California*, October 30, 1863.
9. Mare Island Naval Shipyard Log and *Alta California*, November 13, 1863.
10. Ibid., [November 3, 1863, Comdt. of MINSY advised SECNAV of arrival of another Russian vessel for repairs (Letters Sent)].
11. Ibid.
12. Described in *Solano Herald*, December 15, 1855.
13. *Evening Daily Bulletin*, November 8, 1863.
14. Mare Island Naval Shipyard Memo of November 10, 1863, in Letters Sent.
15. Popov letter from San Francisco, November 11, 1863.
16. Mare Island Naval Shipyard, Letters Sent.
17. Lott, *A Long Line of Ships*, op. cit., 83.
18. Popov letter, November 19, 1863.
19. Lyndall Baker Landauer, *Beyond the Lagoon: A Biography of Charles Melville Scammon* (San Francisco: Associates of the J. Porter Shaw Library, 1986), 76.
20. *Alta California*, November 13, 1863.
21. Ibid., November 24, 1863.
22. Ibid., December 15, 1863.
23. Lott, *A Long Line of Ships*, op. cit., 83.
24. Secretary of the Navy, letter, December 31, 1863.
25. *Alta California*, January 9, 1864.
26. Ibid., January 10, 1864.
27. Golder, "The Russian Fleet and the Civil War," op. cit., 809.
28. *Alta California*, February 14, 1864.
29. Ibid., February 15, 1864.
30. Ibid., February 19, 1864.
31. Ibid., March 8, 1964.
32. Ibid., February 15, 1864.
33. Ibid., February 17, 1864.
34. Ibid., February 20, 1864.
35. Ibid., February 23, 1864.
36. Ibid., February 24, 1864.

37. Ibid.
38. Ibid., March 3, 1864.
39. Ibid., March 6, 1864.
40. San Francisco *Chronicle*, March 5, 1905.
41. Lott, *A Long Line of Ships*, op. cit., 83.
42. Popov letter, March 8, 1864.
43. Popov letter, March 21, 1864.

Chapter 5: The Russian Ball

1. *Alta California*, November 19, 1863.
2. Ibid., November 18, 1863.
3. *Evening Daily Bulletin*, November 18, 1863.
4. *Alta California*, November 19, 1863.
5. Ibid., November 20, 1863.
6. *New York Times*, January 10, 1864.
7. *Evening Daily Bulletin*, November 18, 1863.
8. *Alta California*, December 4, 1863.
9. *Daily Morning Call*, December 25, 1863.

Chapter 6: Final Days

1. *Morskoi Sbornik*, October 1914.
2. Sebastion Dabovich, article published in the Russian Orthodox Messenger (*Russko-Amerikanskii Pravolslavnii*) 2, (1987–98): no. 2, 43 ff. Reprinted in various publications repeatedly. That congregation, initially named St. Alexander Nevsky, received its present name of Holy Trinity in November of 1897.
3. Bolkhovitinov, *Russko-Amerikanskie Otnosherniia* (1990): 132, cited in Lydia T. Black, *Russians in Alaska 1732–1867* (Fairbanks: University of Alaska Press, 2004), 288.
4. Hector Chevigny, *Russian America: The Great Alaskan Venture, 1741–1867* (Portland, OR: Binford and Mort Publishing, 1998), 247.
5. Florence Kern, *The United States Revenue Cutters in the Civil War* (Bethesda, MD: Alised Enterprises, 1990), 2–12.

6. Letter from Bell to Welles, June 23, 1864.
7. *Alta California*, May 21, 1864.
8. *Daily Morning Call*, May 24, 1864.
9. *Alta California*, May 31, 1864.
10. Ibid., June 19, 1864.
11. Ibid., June 25, 1864.
12. Ibid., July 5, 1864.
13. *Daily Morning Call*, July 6, 1864.
14. Ibid., June 29, 1864.
15. Ibid., July 14, 1864.
16. *Alta California*, June 29, 1864.
17. Ibid., August 13, 1864.

Epilogue

1. Joseph F. Loubat, *Gustavus Fox's Mission to Russia 1866.* Originally published as *Narrative of the Mission to Russia, in 1866, of the Hon. Gustavus Vasa Fox* (New York: Arno Press and the *New York Times*, 1970), 88–90.
2. Ibid., 101.
3. Ibid., 233.
4. Ibid., 292.
5. Ibid., 378.
6. Eugene Alexandrov, "This Is How It Was When Russia and the USA Were Friends" *Russian American* (Fall 1997): 199-200.
7. Ian Thompson, *Daily Republic*, January 26, 1994.

BIBLIOGRAPHY

Primary Sources
Daily Alta California
Daily Morning Call
Daily Evening Bulletin
New York Times
Sacramento Union

Log Book of U.S. Revenue Cutter *Shubrick*, Records of the
    U.S. Coast Guard, Record Group 26. National Archives
    and Records Administration, Washington, D.C.
Navy Department, *Official Records of the Union and Confed-
    erate Navies in the War of the Rebellion*, series 1, 27
    vols.; series 2, 3 vols. (Washington, DC, 1894–1922).
Records of Naval Districts and Shore Establishments: Mare
    Island Naval Shipyard. Record Group 181; National
    Archives and Records Administration Building, San
    Bruno, CA.
Russian State Historic Navy Archive, fond 410, St. Peters-
    burg, Russia.
Scammon Papers, Bancroft Library, University of California,
    Berkeley.

Secondary Sources

Adamov, E. A. "Russia and the United States at the Time of the Civil War." *Journal of Modern History* 2, no. 4 (December 1930).

Adams, Ephraim Douglass. *Great Britain and the American Civil War*. New York: Russell and Russell, 1924.

Alexandrov, Eugene. "This Is How It Was When Russia and the USA Were Friends."*The Russian American*, no. 21 (Fall 1997).

Anderson, Bern. *By Sea and By River: The Naval History of the Civil War*. New York: Knopf, 1962.

Andrews, C. L. *The Story of Sitka*. Seattle, WA: Lowman and Hanford, 1922.

Ardinger, Robert Hall. "Implications of the Civil War in California: 1861–1865." MA thesis, La Verne College, 1970.

Bailey, Thomas A. *America Faces Russia: Russian-American Relations from Early Times to Our Day*. Ithaca, NY: Cornell University Press, 1950.

———. "The Russian Fleet Myth Re-Examined." *Mississippi Valley Historical Review* 38 (1951): 81–90.

Balch, Thomas Willing. *The Alabama Arbitration*. Philadelphia: Allen, Lane and Scott, 1900.

Bancroft, Hubert H. *History of California, 1860–1890*. Vol. 7. San Francisco: History Company, 1890.

Bell, Horace. *Reminiscences of a Ranger, or Early Times in Southern California*. Santa Barbara, CA: Wallace Hebberd, 1927.

Bemis, Samuel Flagg. *A Diplomatic History of the United States*. New York: Holt, Rinehart and Winston, 1963.

Black, Lydia T. *Russians in Alaska 1732–1867*. Fairbanks: University of Alaska Press, 2004.

Bloomfield, Howard V. L. *The Compact History of the United States Coast Guard*. New York: Hawthorn Books, 1968.

Bolkhovitinov, Nikolai N. *The Beginnings of Russian-American Relations 1775–1815*. Cambridge, MA: Harvard University Press, 1975.

Boynton, Charles B. *The History of the Navy During the Rebellion.* Vol. 1. New York: D. Appleton, 1867.

Canney, Donald L. *Lincoln's Navy: The Ships, Men and Organization, 1861–65.* Annapolis, MD: Naval Institute Press, 1998.

———. *U.S. Coast Guard and Revenue Cutters, 1790–1935.* Annapolis, MD: Naval Institute Press, 1995.

Carson, James F. "California: Gold to Help Finance the War." *Journal of the West* 14, no. 1 (January 1975).

Chandler, Robert J., ed. *California and the Civil War.* Berkeley, CA: Okeanos Press, 1992.

Chevigny, Hector. *Russian America: The Great Alaskan Venture, 1741–1867.* Portland, OR: Binford and Mort, 1998.

Cogar, William B. *Dictionary of Admirals of the U.S. Navy, 1862–1900.* Vol. 1. Annapolis, MD: Naval Institute Press, 1989.

Cutter, Horace F. "Russia and America." *Overland Monthly* 20 (September 1892): 311–313.

De Arnaud, Charles A. *The Union, and Its Ally, Russia.* Washington, DC: Gibson, 1890.

Delahaye, Tom. "The Bilateral Effect of the Visit of the Russian Fleet in 1863." *Loyola University Student Historical Journal* 15 (Spring–Fall, 1984).

Delgado, James P. *Alcatraz: The Story Behind the Scenery.* Las Vegas, NV: KC Publications, 1985.

Demarest, Peter E. "The Remarkable Career of the Lighthouse Tender *Shubrick.*" *Nautical Research Journal* (March 2001).

Dyer, Brainerd. "Confederate Naval and Privateering Activities in the Pacific." *Pacific Historical Review* 3 (1934): 433–443.

Earle, John J. "The Sentiment of the People of California with Respect to the Civil War." *American Historical Association* (1907).

Ellison, Joseph W. *California and the Nation: 1850–1869.* New York: Da Capo Press, 1969.

Evans, Stephen H. *The United States Coast Guard 1790–1915*. Annapolis, MD: Naval Institute Press, 1949.

Fedorova, Svetlana G., *The Russian Population in Alaska and California: Late 18th Century–1867*. Translated by Richard A. Pierce and Alton S. Donnelly. Kingston, Ontario: Limestone Press, 1973.

Finch, Boyd. "Sherod Hunter and the Confederates in Arizona." *Journal of Arizona History* 10, no. 3 (Autumn 1969): 139–206.

Fowler, Jr., William M. *Under Two Flags: The American Navy in the Civil War*. New York: W. W. Norton, 1990.

Freeze, Gregory. *Russia: A History*. New York: Oxford University Press, 1997.

Gardiner, Robert, ed. *Conway's All the World's Fighting Ships, 1860–1905*. London: Conway Maritime Press, 1979.

Gilbert, Benjamin F. "California and the Civil War." *California Historical Society Quarterly* 40, no. 4 (December 1961): 289–307.

———. "The Confederate Minority in California." *California Historical Society Quarterly* 20, no. 2 (June 1941): 145–165.

———. "Kentucky Privateers in California." *Register of the Kentucky Historical Society* 38, no. 124 (July 1940): 256–266.

———. *Naval Operations in the Pacific, 1861–1866*. PhD diss., University of California, Berkley, 1951.

———. "The Salvador Pirates." *Civil War History* 5, no. 3 (September 1959): 294–307.

———. "San Francisco Harbor Defense During the Civil War." *California Historical Society Quarterly* 31, no. 3 (September 1954).

———. "Welcome to the Czar's Fleet." *California Historical Society Quarterly* 26 (March 1947): 13–19.

Golder, Frank A. "The Russian Fleet and the Civil War," *American Historical Review*, 20 (1915): 801–812.

————. "The American Civil War Through the Eyes of a Russian Diplomat." *American Historical Review* 26 (1921): 454–463.

————. "Russian-American Relations During the Crimean War." *American Historical Review* 31, no. 3 (1926): 462–476.

Gorshkov, Sergei G. *Red Star Rising at Sea*. Translated by Theodore Neely, Jr. Annapolis, MD: Naval Institute Press, 1974.

Hamersly, Lewis R. *The Records of Living Officers of the U.S. Navy and Marine Corps*. Philadelphia: Lippincott, 1870.

Hare, Lloyd C. M. *Salted Tories: The Story of the Whaling Fleets of San Francisco*. Mystic, CT: Marine Historical Association, 1960.

Harpending, Asbury. *The Great Diamond Hoax*. San Francisco: Barry, 1913.

Hawkins, General Rush C. "The Coming of the Russian Ships in 1863." *North American Review* 178 (1904).

Hittell, John S. *A History of San Francisco*. San Francisco: Bancroft, 1878.

Hunt, Aurora. "The Civil War on the Western Seaboard." *Civil War History* 9, no. 2 (June 1963).

————. *The Army of the Pacific*. Glendale, CA: Clark, 1951.

Hunt, Rockwell D., and Nellie Van De Grift Sánchez. *A Short History of California*. New York: Crowell, 1929.

Jane, Fred T. *The Imperial Russian Navy: Its Past, Present, and Future*. New York: Thacker, 1899.

Johnson, Robert Erwin. *Thence Round Cape Horn: The Story of United States Naval Forces on Pacific Station, 1818–1923*. Annapolis, MD: Naval Institute Press, 1963.

————. *United States Naval Forces on Pacific Station, 1818–1923*. PhD diss., Claremont Graduate School, 1956.

Josephy, Alvin M. *The Civil War in the American West*. New York: Knopf, 1992.

Kaplan, Hymen R. "The U.S. Coast Guard and the Civil War." Naval Institute *Proceedings* 86, no. 8 (August 1960): 40–50.

Kern, Florence. *The United States Revenue Cutters in the Civil War*. Bethesda, MD: Alised Enterprises, 1990.

Kern, Florence, and Barbara Voulgaris. *Traditions: 200 Years of History*. Washington, DC: U.S. Coast Guard Public Affairs, n.d.

Kibby, Leo P. *California, the Civil War, and the Indian Problem: An Account of California's Participation in the Great Conflict*. Los Angeles: Morrison and Morrison, 1967.

————. "Some Aspects of California's Military Problems During the Civil War." *Civil War History* 5, no. 3 (September 1959): 251–262.

Kushner, Howard I. "The Russian Fleet and the American Civil War: Another View." *Historian* 34, no. 4 (August 1972).

Landauer, Lyndall Baker. *Beyond the Lagoon: A Biography of Charles Melville Scammon*. San Francisco: Associates of the J. Porter Shaw Library, 1986.

Laurentz, Patrick. "Visit of the Russian Squadrons in 1863." Naval Institute *Proceedings* (May 1935): 692–696.

Lemmon, Sue, and E. D. Wichels. *Sidewheelers to Nuclear Power*. Annapolis, MD: Naval Institute Press, 1977.

Lewis, Oscar. *The War in the Far West: 1861–1865*. Garden City, NJ: Doubleday, 1961.

Lott, Arnold S. *A Long Line of Ships: Mare Island's Century of Naval Activity in California*. Annapolis, MD: Naval Institute Press, 1954.

Loubat, Joseph F. *Gustavus Fox's Mission to Russia 1866*. Originally published as *Narrative of the Mission to Russia, in 1866, of the Hon. Gustavus Vasa Fox*. New York: Arno Press and the *New York Times*, 1970.

Love, Robert W. *History of the U.S. Navy, 1775–1941*. Harrisburg, PA: Stackpole Books, 1992.

Luraghi, Raimondo. *A History of the Confederate Navy*. Annapolis, MD: Naval Institute Press, 1996.

Mahin, Dean B. *One War at a Time: The International Dimensions of the American Civil War*. Washington, DC: Brassey's, 1999.

Maksutov, Jr., Dimitrii. *Sbergov Ameriki: Iubileinvi Istorsicheskii Sbornik* (*The Shores of America; Jubilee Historical Collection*). New York: Association of Former Russian Naval Officers in America, 1939.

Malkin, M. M. *Grazhdansakaia Voima v SshA & Tsarskaia Russiia* (*The Civil War in the U.S.A. and Tsarist Russia*). Moscow/Leningrad: OGIZ, 1939.

Marshall, Amy K. "A History of Buoys and Tenders." USCG *Commandant's Bulletin* (November 1995).

Marshall, Norman S. "Protecting the Gold." *Los Angeles West erners Corral* (Winter 1998): 13–15.

Martini, John A. *Fort Point: Sentry at the Golden Gate*. San Francisco: Golden Gate National Park Association, 1991.

———. *Fortress Alcatraz: Guardian of the Golden Gate*. Kailua, HI: Pacific Monograph, 1990.

Mason, Jack. *Point Reyes: The Solemn Land*. Iverness, CA: North Shore Books, 1970.

McDonald, Lucille. "Revenue Cutter Joseph Lane." *The Sea Chest: Journal of the Puget Sound Maritime Historical Society* 9, no. 1 (September 1975): 16–21.

McPherson, James M. *Battle Cry of Freedom: The Civil War Era*. New York: Oxford University Press, 1988.

Miller, Nathan. *The U.S. Navy: A History*. Annapolis, MD: Naval Institute Press, 1997.

Mitchell, Donald W. *A History of Russian and Soviet Sea Power*. New York: MacMillan, 1974.

Mitchell, Mairin. *The Maritime History of Russia, 1848–1948*. London: Sidgwick and Jackson, 1949.

Mooney, James L., ed. *Dictionary of American Naval Fight ing Ships*. 8 vols. Washington, DC: Naval Historical Center, 1959–1991.

Musicant, Ivan. *Divided Waters: The Naval History of the Civil War*. New York: HarperCollins, 1995.

Nagengast, William E. "The Visit of the Russian Fleet to the United States: Were Americans Deceived?" *Russian Review* 8 (1949): 46–55.

Nash, Jr., Howard P. *A Naval History of the Civil War*. New York: A. S. Barnes, 1972.

Natale, Valerie. "Angel Island: 'Guardian of the Western Gate.'" *Prologue: Quarterly of the National Archives and Records Administration* 30, no. 2 (Summer 1998).

Noble, Dennis L. "Southwest Pacific: A Brief History of U.S. Coast Guard Operations." USCG *Commandant's Bulletin*: 5–89.

Peterson, Douglas. *U.S. Lighthouse Tenders, 1840–1939*. Annapolis, MD: Eastwind Publishing, 2000.

Pierce, Richard A. "Prince D. P. Maksutov: Last Governor of Russian America." *Journal of the West* 6, no. 3 (July 1967): 395–416.

———. *Russian America: A Biographical Dictionary*. Fairbanks, AK: Limestone Press, 1990.

Pomeroy, Earl S. "The Myth After the Russian Fleet, 1863." *New York History* 31, no. 1 (April 1950): 169–176.

———. "The Visit of the Russian Fleet in 1863." *New York History* 24 (October 1943): 512–517.

Riesenberg, Jr., Felix. *Golden Gate: The Story of San Francisco Harbor*. New York: Knopf, 1940.

Ringle, Dennis J. *Life in Mr. Lincoln's Navy*. Annapolis, MD: Naval Institute Press, 1998.

Sandburg, Carl. *Abraham Lincoln: The Prairie Years and the War Years*. Pleasantville, NY: Reader's Digest Association, 1970.

Saul, Norman E. *Distant Friends: The United States and Russia, 1763–1867*. Lawrence: University Press of Kansas, 1991.

Seton-Watson, Hugh. *The Russian Empire, 1801–1917*. Oxford: Clarendon Press, 1967.

Shaw, David W. *Sea Wolf of the Confederacy: The Daring Civil War Raids of Naval Lt. Charles W. Read*. New York: Free Press, 2004.

Sideman, Bell Becker, and Lillian Friedman, eds. *Europe Looks at the Civil War*. New York: Collier, 1962.

Siegel, Adam B. *The Wartime Diversion of U.S. Navy Forces in Response to Public Demands for Augmented Coastal Defense*. Professional Paper 472. Alexandria, VA: Center for Naval Analyses, November 1989.

Silverstone, Paul H. *Civil War Navies, 1855–1883*. Annapolis, MD: Naval Institute Press, 2001.

Soley, James Russell. *The Navy in the Civil War, Vol. 1: The Blockade and the Cruisers*. New York: Scribner's, 1883.

Spaulding, Imogene. "The Attitude of California to the Civil War." PhD diss., University of Southern California, 1912.

Sprout, Harold, and Margaret Sprout. *The Rise of American Naval Power 1776–1918*. Annapolis, MD: Naval Institute Press, 1966.

Stern, Philip Van Doren. *When the Guns Roared*. Garden City, NY: Doubleday, 1965.

Straus, Oscar S. "The United States and Russia: Their Historical Relations." *North American Review* 181 (1905).

Strobridge, Truman R. *The United States Coast Guard and the Civil War: The U.S. Revenue Marine, Its Cutters and Semper Paratus*. Washington, DC: U. S. Coast Guard Public Affairs Division, 1972.

Tenny, W. J. *The Military and Naval History of the Rebellion in the United States*. New York: D. Appleton, 1866.

Tinkman, George H. *California: Men and Events*. Stockton: Record Publishing, 1915.

Tucker, Spencer C. *A Short History of the Civil War at Sea*. Wilmington, DE: Scholarly Resources, 2002.

U.S. Coast Guard Academy. "The Shubrick Incident." *Alumni Association Bulletin* (March 1941).

Watford, W. H. "The Far-Western Wing of the Rebellion, 1861–1865." *California Historical Society Quarterly* 34, no. 2 (June 1955).

Watts, Anthony J. *The Imperial Russian Navy*. London: Arms and Armour, 1990.

Weldin, G. C. "Visit of the Russian Squadrons in 1863." *Naval Institute Proceedings* (December 1935).

West, Jr., Richard S. *Mr. Lincoln's Navy*. New York: Longmans, Green, 1957.

White, Jr., Richard D. "Saga of the Side-Wheeled Steamer *Shubrick*." *The American Neptunem* 34, no. 1 (Spring 1976).

Wilson, Timothy. *Flags at Sea*. Annapolis, MD: Naval Institute Press, 1999.

Woldman, Albert A. *Lincoln and the Russians*. Cleveland: World Publishing, 1952.

INDEX

ABOUT THE AUTHOR

Dr. C. Douglas Kroll is an assistant professor of history at the College of the Desert in Palm Desert, California.

Born in Florence, South Carolina, Dr. Kroll grew up in Lanark, Illinois. He graduated with a B.S. degree from the U.S. Coast Guard Academy in 1971 and served as a coast guard officer afloat and overseas before resigning his commission to become a navy chaplain. He retired in 1996 as a commander in the naval reserve. He holds a M.Div. from Luther Theological Seminary (St. Paul, MN), a M.A. in history from the University of San Diego, and a Ph.D. in history from the Claremont Graduate University and is the author of numerous articles dealing with coast guard and naval history. His book, *Commodore Ellsworth P. Bertholf: First Commandant of the Coast Guard*, was named the "Best Book on Coast Guard History" by the Foundation for Coast Guard History in 2004.

Prior to coming to College of the Desert, he taught at California Polytechnic University-Pomona, California State University-Los Angeles, Azusa Pacific University, the University of La Verne, and Mt. San Jacinto College. Dr. Kroll has been a full-time faculty member at College of the Desert since the fall of 2001.

Doug and his wife Lana make their home in Palm Desert and have two grown sons: Timothy, who lives Placentia, California and works for the Orange County Court System, and Matthew, serving in the U.S. Coast Guard.